MW00935049

Rapture:

Could There Be More Than One?

by

Dr. Scott Young

Dr. Scott Young

Copyright © 2017 by Dr. Scott Young

Rapture: Could There Be More than One?

www.DrScottYoung.com

This book is a work of non-fiction. This Book/eBook is licensed for your personal enjoyment only and may not be re-sold or given away to other people. If you like to share this book with another person, please purchase an additional copy for each person.

The Bible verses are taken from the amazing HCSB (the Holman Christian Standard Bible) with incredible abilities to save notes, read the Greek and Hebrew wording and study the Word. It is available from LifeWay.com, the Apple App store, and the Android app store.

All rights reserved, including the right to reproduce this book or portions thereof, in any form. No part of this text may be reproduced in any form without the express written permission of the author.

All rights reserved.

ISBN-13: 978-17264656

ISBN-10: 172649659

Rapture: Could There Be More than One?

INTRO

Why do we talk about the Rapture? What is the world's clock ticking down to? Such a common questions play into the thoughts of most Americans and many around the world. You likely have noticed the significant rise in Post-Apocalyptic films and television shows. Everyone wants to know how the world will end, and if we will we survive.

The Bible offers true answers to these questions, but many have misinterpreted those responses. While some students of the End Times were attempting to find the answers, they trusted someone else's interpretation instead of receiving it "straight from the horse's mouth," as my dad used to say.

As we read Scripture, we find that truth is available to all people. God wants us to know what is going to happen in the End Times. We will answer one of the biggest questions: "Is the Rapture even in the Bible?" In this Eschatology study, we will investigate the Rapture as this is one of the most recognizable terms when we are referring to *The End*.

Also let the reader note that I **bold** a few beginning statements in later chapters. This is to remind you as to the groups and the concepts that are vital in understanding. Most of you will have heard of the concepts within this book. I pray that your mind is opened to the understanding I am explaining in the Word.

Jeff Swanson, of whom we will discuss later on, is a close friend in ministry. When I took him, I had a strong prompting of the Holy Spirit to a Prophecy in the News conference in which I believed that he was supposed to speak at even though he didn't have a specific invite. When he was asked to take one of the speaker's spots who didn't show up for the conference, there was a hush over the room as he introduced some of these topics. The Holy Spirit was moving among more than 450 people there that day in Orlando, Florida. The statements from the people in the booth we had for his ministry were centered upon that they had never heard this information. The freedom they felt from the sharing of this Biblical unification of the Eschatology I will present in this book allowed a breath of fresh air to the Spirits of those in that room. This is my prayer for you.

Table of Contents

Chapter 1

MY JOURNEY INTO ESCATOLOGY

I had a friend from high school named Scott, and for me who can't always remember names, his was easy to recall. Scott is the older brother of my best friend, Eric, whom I have kept up with since those high school days, more than thirty-five years ago. Scott was struggling in his relationship with the Lord when I reconnected with him years later. This was a surprise to me since Scott, one grade ahead of me, had been bold in his faith at Douglas County High School in Castle Rock, Colorado. So, I began to dialogue with Scott about his life since those school days. I don't remember how we started the next topic, but I do recall Scott blurting out, "You know the Bible doesn't even mention a Rapture."

For a person who has researched Eschatology (the Study of Biblical End Times), I was taken aback and frankly didn't follow where he was heading with his retort to a belief doctrine known as the Rapture. We discussed it further, but at that time, Scott didn't want to be dissuaded from his path that the Bible was a thing of his youth that he had put away. Scott came back stronger than ever in his faith years later, but I never forgot his Rapture comment; it is one that I have heard many times since.

The Rapture of the Church and its timing is a hotly debated topic among Believers and a powerful point of derision among non-believers in Jesus. Some will ask, especially at Prophecy Conferences, "Are you a Pre-Tribber (belief in a Pre-Tribulation Rapture)?" This question alone allows the individual to know if they are on the same side of the fence or not; whether they are about to debate the other on the error of his ways; or to go down a theological brotherhood path of mutual agreement. The situation is tantamount to telling another football fan that you are a Dallas Cowboy's fan. You immediately find out if you are cheering for the same side!

Almost every other religion, the well-recognized ones such as Mormonism, Islam or Jehovah's Witnesses, speak of a Last Set of Days, about ways that the world will end, and how their god contrives the answers to all the earth's problems. Ultimately, the truest Believers to their sect are reconciled to Him in a righteousness born of the adherence to the laws and a fear of what their God might do to them if they disobey. The God of the Old and New Testaments has a far different path to the End than that of other false religions.

When I was a boy, I didn't read as well as others did. I couldn't even accomplish the simple task of skipping when I was in first grade. Only in college did I find out that Dyslexia, a neurological condition where the letters and/or the words are perceived to be backwards when interpreted by the visual cortex, was the diagnosis that placed me in the *Extra Help* class. I hated it, feeling that I was on the short bus and dumber than the rest of my class. No child wants to be singled out in those formative years. Only later in high school did I learn to love words. While procuring a degree in English, I took on the toughest portions of a Dyslexic's processing of words. It was then that I began to develop a love for writing that became stronger through the years as I studied for my Master's, then Doctorate in Audiology. During my later degree program, I was trying to bring my free-form writing style into a curt style of prose, a form I still don't like to discard when writing technical literature.

As I said, my disability kept me from any enjoyment in reading until I was a sixteen. I picked up Hal Lindsey's *The Late Great Planet Earth* in 1982. I will ever be grateful to the man for writing a book that changed my educational and Biblical study habits. Throughout high school and college, I began to devour any book on Eschatology. As a college freshman, I took on the task to read through the Bible in one college year. I fell in love with the Bible in all of its nuances throughout the decades. I kept reading and rereading any of the End Time passages, because my generation was supposed to end with Orson Wells' depiction of *1984*. I couldn't believe that we would live much longer on the earth and had this sneaking suspicion that Jesus was coming back soon. I came to realize that the writers of the Epistles, especially Paul, had that same connotation that God's timetable was almost at an end. But yet, here we are today.

So, how can we still trust in a book that says Jesus is coming back soon? He didn't come back in Paul's day (early in that first century AD), and He hasn't returned yet in my lifetime. There is a difference between "immanence" and something that is about to happen tomorrow. If I say that I intend to vacation in Denver, that doesn't mean that I am going to come tomorrow, just that I am going to do it. Yet when God says He is coming back to the earth, some of us assume it means tomorrow. In fact, it may be tomorrow, but you can be assured that He WILL be back! I think the readers of prophecy need to see the perspective of a timeless God versus a time-locked human thought process. Immanence means that He is coming in a time that we really don't know, or that we cannot nail down the date, and doesn't mean that *He* doesn't know it.

A fascinating verse to which most prophecy speakers don't often refer is Revelation 9:15 in which John stipulates that the four angels were released for this "hour, day, month and year." It is the only place in the Bible that Jesus that gives a very specific observation of the precise moment within history for the occurrence of the Sixth Trumpet, or any other moment in time. Therefore, we can conclude that what Jesus unveiled to John in this amazing book of Revelation was stating that there is a peculiar future time for His plans. The passage above is not stating the *date* of the Rapture but of the event of the Sixth Trumpet which is years into the Tribulation.

Have you asked yourself why Jesus didn't use a Scripture to discuss the actual date or even a potential timeframe of the Rapture? He simply didn't want us to focus on the date. That is consistent in Matthew 24 and other scriptures indicating our level of trust in Him for the exact future. If I knew that I was going to die 20 years from now, would I respond differently to today? You bet I would. Jesus didn't reveal the moment of time in which He was going to start the timeclock of the end of days for humanity, or the date that He would step upon the earth. But He referenced a point in time approximately eighteen months to the end of the Tribulation inside of the Sixth Trumpet. Do we know that for sure? No, it's an estimate; but the approximation isn't the point. Jesus wants His creation to trust in the One who made them and not determine the date of history's end.

Consider that before the foundation of the earth, God set up hundreds of prophecies that Jesus was to fulfill including one of my favorites, the Bethlehem Star. There is a website I highly recommend regarding to learn more about this topic, www.BethlehamStar.net. In the analysis, a lawyer named Frederick Larson indicates with near certainty that the Star was set to a specific timeframe exactly as Matthew indicated in his writings. God had a stopwatch for Jesus' first coming and based on hundreds of fulfilled prophesies including the Star, we can be assured that He will be right on time for His second coming.

During my freshman and sophomore years in college, I took on personal tasks to prove numerous topics in the Bible were true. With my Bible in one hand and a notebook in the other, I scribbled my theories directly from my study of the NIV pages. I studied Jesus' death and resurrection, the Shroud of Turin, Secular Rock Music, Backward Masking, and many other topics. I led an InterVarsity Christian Fellowship Bible Study even into grad school. I hated being told that we had to teach from pre-printed Bible studies that we as student leaders should follow. So, my custom-created lessons were all mostly verse by verse, leading fellow students through my favorite passages of Scripture. Years later, my father-in-law asked me if I thought that I had missed my calling to be a Pastor or Teacher instead of a Doctor of Audiology. I told him that I could be a good Audiologist and a good Bible teacher at the same time.

My passion is to write about the Lord, and how my brain perceives His world. Some of my prose is based in the fictional realm following a few characters through specific periods of time, while other portions of my writing happen to be non-fictional.

It was while I was writing another fictional novel set in one of my favorite historical periods, World War II, that I felt derailed by the Lord to put that piece aside in order to tackle another the topic of which I taught at St. James Church in Tulsa, Oklahoma. I believe God called me to discuss the End Times. Therein, I present this treatise on the *Rapture: Could There Be More than One?*

Chapter 2

WHAT IS THE RAPTURE?

To begin, we need to launch into a conversation about the word *Rapture*. Some don't even believe that a Rapture, a "catching away" as literally translated in the Greek, is even a possibility for the Church. Others have never heard of the concept, partially because the actual word "Rapture" is not found in the Bible, and references to the action of the *Catching Away* in the last book of the Bible are a relatively difficult set of wordings to read. The whole topic of Eschatology is so divisive to some churches that they ignore that the Bible even talks about it. Actually, as much as thirty percent of the Word indicates an ending to the world. Shouldn't that be teaching upon the End Times at least as many Sundays (I'd even settle for a couple months of Sundays)?

Many people discount and even mock those that look forward to being taken from this worsening world to our forever home, Heaven. However, while the word *Rapture* is not translated as such in the New Testament, a Rapture event is certainly described. So, how do we address Scott's statement to me all those years ago? The *Rapture* is mentioned, by my own counting, more than thirty-nine times in New

Testament verses.

My close friend, Jeff Swanson, has invested thirty years studying Scripture in order to create a verse by verse chronology Bible (www.PlanBible.com). His organization, Jeff Swanson Ministries, offers the best Eschatology-based Bible of which I know. No other Bible even attempts to, for example, organize all the references of King David in the Old Testament in a sequence of events. He absolutely does not change any of the words, but with the aid of at least two outside and verifiable historical references he indicates the correct placement of each verse.

Jeff and I have talked in depth regarding End Time issues. Our wives state categorically that they sometimes need to separate us since we will converse longer to one another than to anyone they know. Jeff's work gives incredibly ordered references to Eschatology, while keeping the uniqueness of the document all the way from the Creation and the End Time events of the Bible.

The Greek word, *Rapture,* comes from the word *Harpazo.* I Thessalonians 4:16-18 presents an inside theological view of the Pre-Tribulational Rapture of the Church. The best way to explain this is to use the analogy of a chess game.

As I grew up, I thought that I was relatively good at playing chess. Very few of my family or friends could beat me in my teen years. As my own son began to reach for a board, I coaxed him along in the basics of the game and allowed him to beat me at first so as not to discourage him from playing.

At some point, I noted that he could beat me so effectively that he was becoming sympathetic to my bogus moves with groans of "Oh dad, I am sorry that I took that rook." But sometimes my competitive side got the better of me and in the unlikely event that I was able to take his queen off the board, I would *snatch* the piece with such alacrity that he could hardly identify which piece I took away!

The word *Harpazo* has this same connotation. It means that God is going to come in the clouds to remove His Church, *snatching them up* from the jaws of this world and repurposing them *for another destiny.* In ancient times, this word was used nefariously such as when a man took another woman for his own sexual desires, spiriting her away from her family. Christ, our Bridegroom, will not snatch His Bride away, the Church, in any nefarious way. It will be a holy, exciting and glorious event! The Bible gives all the different sides to the argument of the Rapture – pre, mid and post – which we will be covering in the chapters ahead.

A phrase I learned during my college years from our Baptist Student Union Campus Pastor John Mark was "the Old Testament is the New Testament concealed, and the New Testament is the Old Testament revealed." I have quoted that so many times that my family can repeat it verbatim. In addition to its many layers of knowledge, we can view the Old Testament as a mirror of New Testament events.

For example, the Old Testament High Priest Melchizedek was a forerunner, or a mirror of the High Priest, we find fulfilled in Jesus Christ of the New Testament. In Genesis 14, Abraham set up the example to give a tithe to the priests (ten percent of our bounty). Christians today bring to the storehouse 10% of their increase as well in tithes.

Then we have Enoch who was a perfect example of a Rapture event. In Genesis 5, we meet Enoch who was a relatively young man before he went off to be with God at 365 years old. In Genesis 5:24 "Enoch walked with God: then he was not there because God took him." Some claim that Enoch was killed by God stating that the Bible is not clear on its wording. This simply isn't the case. The word here is *Laqah* in Aramaic. It means to fetch, carry away, marry or be seized. The word's connotation is mysteriously similar to the *Harpazo* utilized by Paul in the New Testament. The resemblance of the wording could not be clearer. God took Enoch home to be with him in a type of Rapture. The old Jewish customs of marriage reveal to us much of how they thought about the bride and her role inside the response to her groom. The Bride is Ephesians' connotation of the Church. Some American traditions actually are brought over from those early views of how a ceremony should proceed, of which we will deal in Chapter 17.

In II Kings 2, we read the story of Elijah being taken up into heaven by a chariot. The story is one of the most fantastic the Bible records. It affects Elisha in his future ministry and reveals a second person in the Old Testament who does not experience death. These two men, Enoch and Elijah, have their Body, Spirit and Soul translated into Heaven without experiencing the bodily decay. I believe that this is a type and shadow of the conversion that we will see in the future that concerns our Soul and Spirit.

Chapter 3

PRE-TRIBULATION RAPTURE

The term, Pre-Tribulation Rapture, considers that the Believer is extracted from the earth out of this reality before the beginning of the ugliness called the Tribulation, a seven year time period. In this view, the Church is waiting for Jesus to come into the clouds and take his Bride to be with Him sometime before the beginning of the Tribulation. A misunderstood point by some of the Church is that the Tribulation begins with the Rapture of the Church. Daniel 9:27 clearly states that "He will make a firm covenant with many for one week, but in the middle of the week he will put a stop to sacrifice and offering. The abomination of desolation will be on a wing of the temple until the decreed destruction is poured out on the desolator (HCSB)." The second part of the verse in Daniel is discussing the middle of the Tribulation, and what the Anti-Christ will do inside of the temple in Jerusalem, that has yet to be rebuilt. Daniel's Week is a metaphor for seven years.

The first portion of the above verse, on the other hand, delineates that the Anti-Christ must enter into an agreement with the world to save peace in the Middle East, specifically for Israel with many nations included. For those who do not know, the Anti-Christ is a figure of the worst sort of all characters throughout human history. You may believe that the Bible is referring to a mythical personality, but I assure you that Scripture indicates that he will be all too real. He is the embodiment of all that Satan wishes to represent to humanity. The Anti-Christ will initially be viewed as a man of peace. TIME Magazine will probably put him on the cover as the Man of the Year.

I believe that there are reasons for this idea of a peaceful world leader, too numerous to discuss in this book. The reader should flip over to Ezekiel 38 and 39 and its scary global War of Gog and Magog. Concisely stated, in the future, Israel will be attacked by several nations, at which God will rescue His people by several miraculous events. The world will openly wonder about the abilities of Israel. Those nations who attacked Israel will die a horrible fate.

Firstly, all of their soldiers will lie in the deserts just east of Jerusalem. Their remains will wait as many as seven months to be buried. Israel will use the fuel they find from the weapons of war for seven years (which is the common Biblical understanding that this war precedes the Tribulation). The nations who attempt Israel's downfall will also suffer in some way in their own level of punishment. It is my belief that Israel will be empowered by their astonishing victory over many countries; the vanquished will fear that the war path will be an open season for her enemies.

Why will Israel be a power to be reckoned with when they are threatened after the War of Gog and Magog? Each time in the past decades since 1948, Israel has swiftly and brutally chastised their enemies when they have harmed Israel. I believe that this may be the exact reason that the Anti-Christ introduces himself to the world: to keep Israel at bay, away from her frightened opposition. It is this peace treaty that the Anti-Christ brokers that actually begins the Tribulation.

Conversely, it is understood that the Rapture of His Bride would occur sometime before the beginning of the Tribulation. The signing of the peace treaty and the Ezekiel 38-39 war have nothing to do with the Rapture of Jesus' Bride, but the world affairs, which include the peace treaty, will definitely be affected by the Jewish response to being attacked. The Rapture could occur anywhere from weeks to a few years before the announcement of the peace treaty with Israel. Adherents to this Pre-Tribulation Rapture view focus on Christ coming back for them, meaning that they should be ready at any time to *go home.*

Detractors from this perception of the Rapture before the Tribulation indicate many possible problems with this doctrine, but the strongest point is summarized in the following manner: Chinese Christians, for example, have suffered innumerable hardships throughout dozens of years and have never escaped severe persecutions by their government. Why does the Western Church believe that they should not have to endure that same type of pain? Those devotees to anything other than a Pre-Tribulation Rapture specify that suffering produces character (a summary of Romans 5:4) which can only be a good thing for the Western Church to experience, so that they can enter the Kingdom of God pure, righteous, and invigorated to do what Jesus wants us to do.

The problem with the contrary thoughts against the Pre-Tribulational Rapture is that righteousness is not perfected by suffering, a significant difference from the character discussion of Romans 5:4. The word Righteousness in Romans in Greek (*dikaiosyne)* is defined as one who is unable to do wrong. It is not the process of doing right only, that most of the Church believes based upon our own English definition, but Jesus, utilizing the Greek word for Righteousness, had *no ability to do wrong*. This is a much higher standard to attain from the common definition. So, if only Christ can be Righteous, we need His grace to obtain this gold standard of excellence. That is why we cannot compare our ability to create Righteousness with the Bible's conversation therein. My upcoming second book upon *The Truth and Lies of What We Believe* will actually be delineating this concept in severe detail. Look for it on www.DrScottYoung.com.

Now, the character of an individual Believer, on the other hand, can be affected inside of suffering. The Seven-Year Tribulation is a type of affliction that no man upon the earth will ever understand until the world experiences it. That does not mean that suffering doesn't bring strength, and of course it did for Paul who wrote most of the New Testament as well as the Disciples who penned the rest of it. But the Tribulation is on an infinitely different level of carnage than the world has ever known. Matthew 24:22 indicates that if the days of the Tribulation were not shortened, no one would even survive.

There will be Martyrs as a group of people who will die for their faith in the later half of the Tribulation. Their distress will be so immense that the mind cannot imagine, as I have spent time looking at the entirety of the Bible. But the Word indicates that "we are not appointed to wrath..." (I Thess. 5:9). I would countermand those who believe that we need suffering to sustain our Souls that only the Tribulation can bring.

My studies indicate that the first half of the Tribulation, long believed to be relatively peaceful, is much worse than any day prior. The second half of this timeframe will be a virtual hell on earth in which almost all humans will be subject to die horribly. Wrath will be on the rampage. The Pre-Tribulation Rapture of the Church is a blessing given to us when we study the End Times which has been spoken as much as twenty-eight percent of the time in Scripture.

Let me explain it another way. As a small business owner, if you found that I spoke of money and the handling thereof, as much as thirty percent of the time in my company manual, you would rightly discern that it is a critical topic for the success and focus of my company. If, on the other hand, you chose against my view of the handling of cash with my company, then it might not be a good idea to work for me. The Bible spends more than a quarter of its text, New and Old Testaments, upon Eschatology. If we cannot devote the time that God expends on what He believes is important for us to know, then we are missing *His* Scriptural point.

A cursory reading of Revelation 1:3 is spoken by many prophecy teachers, and correctly so, that there is a blessing inside taking Eschatology seriously: "The one who reads this is blessed, and those who hear the words of this prophecy and keep what is written in it are blessed, because the time is near!" But let's get into the Greek to know what that verse is really saying. The key words are *Reads, Hear,* and *Keep.* Reads (*anaginosko*) is much deeper than our superficial flow from word to word. *Read* means to distinguish between and recognize the difference of the wording, of which I might call not just reading but clearly understanding the text.

To Hear (*akouo*) states that we must not just hear the words, but study what it is saying so that we perceive its meaning. We would need to smash together the words *Read* and *Hear,* so that understanding occurs. To Keep (*tereo*) is to watch out for and guard carefully the words of the text. If we distinguish, understand, and guard the words spoken in this book of Revelation, then we have a blessing. You might also consider the word *Keep* as an Apologetic word that we would argue for or contend for that sematic. Then we, therefore, have that blessing that I believe is the Rapture of the Church. Similar wording is repeated in Luke 12:41-48 in which it describes the End Time reward for people who focus on Jesus and His coming. Next, we will otherwise delineate the Mid-Tribulation Rapture.

Chapter 4

MID-TRIBULATION RAPTURE

Pre-Tribulation Rapture – Some believe the Church is removed before the Tribulation.

The people that believe in the Mid-Tribulation Rapture concept are fewer in number than the other ends of the scale since most hold to either the Pre-and Post-Tribulation doctrines. I have counted approximately eleven Scriptures that are most likely a reference to a Mid-Tribulation Rapture but there could also be more (see the Scriptures for all information presented at the end of this book). The Mid-Trib view holds that the Church will be here upon the earth up to the middle of the Tribulation which will then give way to the unbelievers when the hard-core suffering begins. It purports that when the Anti-Christ comes upon the scene at the signing of the peace covenant in Daniel 9:27, he keeps a relatively peaceful world for the initial period of the Tribulation. If the Church doesn't leave the earth before the Tribulation starts, then potentially little prophetic significance would naturally change in this vantage point.

Mid-Tribbers often perceive that their focus should

be upon the Anti-Christ and his identification for the world to beware of his presence. They spend much of their prophecy watching wondering which political and religious leaders could meet up to the qualifications of the Anti-Christ and the False Prophet. They believe that we, as the Church, will easily be able to identify these two men's movements and decrees, because we are studying the Lord's Word. Revelation 13:11-18 indicates that the Anti-Christ and False Prophet originate in a political position from the "sea and the sand." The above analogies indicate that the two massive personalities will originate from obscurity as observed by many prophecy teachers who hold to other than Mid-Trib views and a close reading of the Word. It is not possible to know who the Anti-Christ is before the Tribulation begins, even if only there was a Mid-Tribulational Rapture and no Pre-Tribulational Rapture. Why? Because he is revealed for that future timeframe (2 Thess. 2:7).

The most glaring problem with the Mid-Trib view only is that a tiny group of people will have a mighty impact upon the world as indicated by Scripture. They are called the 144,000 Jews who preach throughout the earth and come on the scene after the peace treaty. Revelation 7:1-9 indicates that they will be responsible for bringing more people than any generation before into the Kingdom. "After this, I looked, and there was a vast multitude from every nation, tribe, people and language, which no one could number, standing before the throne and before the Lamb. They were robed in white with palm branches in their hands."

Utilizing a little English grammar, we see the preamble to the verse, *after this, I looked.* That is a backward reference to the verses beforehand or utilized as a timestamp to the past. These set of sentences are clearly not Pre-Trib Rapture verses (such as Revelation 4:1) which demonstrates that these people are in Heaven after Jesus proclaims to the seven Churches his positive and negative views of their responses to life (Revelation 2 and 3). We also note that *After this I looked* designates that a few of the Seals will already have been opened up in Heaven by Jesus meaning that the Tribulation has begun when you follow the timing of the Revelation coming to chapter 7.

This is one of the most powerful evidences of a Mid-Trib Rapture in the whole of the New Testament, and it was one of the verses that has bothered me for more than thirty years. I had never been able to reconcile it to the rest of Eschatology research; it just didn't fit because of that preamble portion of the verse. That is why most adherents to the Pre-Trib and Post-Trib positions cannot claim dominance over the other. "All Scripture is God breathed approved for teaching, exhortation..." in 2 Timothy 3:16 meaning that we cannot throw the baby out with the bathwater in the Mid-Trib placement of the Rapture.

In fact, these adherents have at times also have pointed to a partial Rapture theory. In their assumption, only the really righteous portion of the Church goes up in the Pre-Trib Rapture, then those who have refined themselves such as examples of the 144K believers go up before the Lord. Again, we reference back to an understanding of how one refines him/herself: would it be by the blood of Jesus or by the works of his/her abilities? Pretty obvious on that one, huh? It's by Jesus' blood atoned from the "foundation of the earth" in Revelation 13:8, and nothing to do with our own ability to be clean.

Revelation 7:9 denotes that every people group, nation and spoken language will be represented who come to know Christ and will stand before the throne in glory. The conundrum is that if the 144,000 are responsible for the greatest evangelism the world has ever imagined, what is our role of the Bride in this deadly timeframe? Or, to say it another way, why wouldn't the Church be mobilized to convert the people of the earth in the massive effectiveness that the 144,000 Jews will do, especially with the idea that the Anti-Christ would be revealed with his False Prophet?

Some use weaker arguments that the Church has been immobilized to accomplish her task; therefore, meaning that a replacement group must be introduced by Jesus to finish the job. There are other interpretations that indicate that the 144,000 will focus on the Jews while the Christians will focus on the Gentiles. This is not what Scripture says, so I therefore cannot Biblically support that claim. Again, the above verse indicates that the 144,000 are directly responsible for every tribe, nation and tongue into a believing knowledge of Jesus.

The singular Mid-Trib Rapture perspective struggles to explain how the Church is discussed through dozens of times from Revelation chapters 1-4, then shows a group that is readily identified as *Believers* in Heaven in chapters 5 through 6. The Book then doesn't mention the Church again until chapter 19. When it does refer to Believers, it conspicuously changes the term to Tribulation Saints (*hagios*). It is not the same term and the study of apologetics has to be applied: Mid-Tribbers never explain this change in wording, nor the real absence of the Church in anyway. I believe in letting the Word explain itself instead of changing it to satisfy anyone's belief about what I want it to say. In the past, I, like some who are reading this book, didn't like the implication of what a Mid and a Pre-Trib Rapture could imply.

Chapter 5

POST-TRIBULATION RAPTURE

Pre-Tribulation Rapture – Some believe the Church is removed before Tribulation.

Mid-Tribulation Rapture – Some believe the Church would be removed in the Middle of the Tribulation.

144,000 Jewish converts will arise in the Tribulation and evangelize the world.

In the last interpretative approach to the Rapture of the Church, Post-Tribulationalists imagine that the Christians will be taken from the earth at the very end of all the 21 judgments of Christ (the Seal, the Trumpet and the Bowl judgments). Adherents to this concept mention, as we discussed earlier, that the Church must be willing to endure hardship to perfect our faith in Jesus, therefore to make us be perfect in His sight when He comes back.

There are points to the logic that are unmistakable and evident in Scripture that are contrary to this idea, including that we are already perfect in our faith and not in what we do, but in whom we believe. Let's be clear on this subject. Is the Church, or any Believer for that matter, perfect in our flesh? Are any of us without sin in our lives? Of course, that makes no sense!

So, what kind of perfection can the Believer have in the Body? To what level of perfection can we achieve in the body that would be acceptable for Christ to come back? I think you are perceiving the pattern of this context. Pastor Bob Yandian said it slightly differently in a podcast regarding the Last Days in 2018. He stated that some believe in that Jesus cannot return until we are unified as the Body of Believers. His reading of the Word indicated that the only time we will accomplish that feat is when we enter into Heaven. I loved that finality of our Sozo (salvation).

We are NEVER perfect in our Body, or shall we say without sin! Our Spirits are seated in Heavenly places (Col. 3:3, Eph. 2:6 and others) so how do we become perfect? In the body we cannot be perfect in any way. We are imperfect and will sin throughout our lives, because we are in the Body. If our Father in Heaven cannot stand the sight of any sin (Romans 3:23 "For all have fallen short of the glory of Christ"), then how is it the body of a live Believer in Jesus going to eradicate sin? This has been an ongoing conundrum for the Church for centuries. I am going to explore this topic further in my "Truth and Lies of What We Believe" series in my second book regarding the concept of Righteousness. Suffice it to say that we are already the righteousness in Christ. There is nothing we could do to accomplish eroding sin in our lives or we would not have needed the Blood of Jesus. Therefore, our job is to follow every day within the footsteps of Christ. Jesus is the author and perfector of the Faith. Ephesians 2:7-8 indicates that we are not supposed to boast in the Lord in what we do, but inside of our Faith in Him. The End Times are clearly not about eradicating our sin and making us perfect.

But there has been a divergence in the last twenty years or so adding a caveat that the Lord will take His Church away from His wrath. They call it Pre-Wrath Rapture ("we are not appointed to wrath..." 1 Thess. 5:9). Some point that, before the most horrible and deadliest judgments upon the face of the earth in which the humans left should be dealt with by an angry God, the Lord will descend to take His Church off the earth for a short respite to spare them from the global wrath of the Lamb! Without defining all the twenty-one judgments listed in Revelation as wrath or not wrath connotations, the question about when the Believers of the world should leave this earth in a Rapture to answer the above Scripture can never be fully explained.

Therefore, denoting what is wrath throughout the whole Bible would be a sticky minefield in the ramblings of the amateur and professional Scriptural scholar to argue as to which portion of the Bible is wrath and which is not into Ad Infinium arguments. I do not choose to spend our time fleshing out each of those judgment points, because the focus is upon the *Who's* not the *What's* in the End. I will conclude that the Post-Trib or Pre-Wrath are on the same level, because they are clearly toward the end of the Tribulation and are definitely not related to the Mid-Trib or a Pre-Trib viewpoint.

Pre Wrath

The Pre-Wrath Rapture theory believes that one can survive upon the earth effectively by hiding out in mountains and secret facilities to protect themselves from all that will come upon the earth. Since the people have studied the potential apocalyptic ends as well as the counteraction of that end, they can navigate the waters of trouble effectively by preparing for the worst that the Lord can bring to this planet. If a survivalist (we will explore this group later on) has considered the ramifications of an Electro-Magnetic Pulse (EMP), they feel that their protections of their electronic gear would allow them to weather the EMP storm that will devastate the rest of humanity. I personally have struggled with this view in their writings, noting that they have significant derision in their arguments against the Pre-Trib escapism that persuades the Church to not prepare for the end. Almost every book with this theological bent gives the indication that those who have a preference toward the Pre-Trib slant are to be treated as an enemy at worst or with dismissiveness at best.

The enigmas regarding the Pre-Wrath standoff are numerous. Where in Scripture is it proposed that we should hide out until Jesus comes back for His Church? Why do the two groups, one called the 144,000 Jews and the other, the Two Witnesses who will be discussed later, complete all the heavy lifting of preaching the gospel when the Church is supposedly doing no priestly good in their duties as Ambassadors for Christ, shivering in their bunkers? Also, believing that the whole period doesn't have a level of wrath associated with it is a misunderstanding of the severity of the beginning three and a half years as well as the depth of human and spiritual depravity that will occur in the second three and a half years.

The deeper I study the topic of the End Times, the more I find that each portion of the Tribulation is worse than any of the most terrifying horror films recorded within the compilation of human thought. In other words, if the first three and a half years of the

Tribulation are not as peaceful as some would have you think; because of the presence of a world leader who is exerting his control over the planet, how in the world can we imagine that the last half is not the worst that man could perceive?

In essence, the nature of the timeframe is to bring mankind out of his stupor, so that he may be able to avoid the second death. God wants all humankind to come to a knowledge of Him that they will call on His name and be saved. That's the message of the New Testament and the purpose of the Tribulation.

Chapter 6

RAPTURE CONDUNDRUM: WHICH ONE IS CORRECT?

Pre-Tribulation Rapture – Some believe the Church is removed before Tribulation.

Mid-Tribulation Rapture – Some believe the Church would be removed in the Middle of the Tribulation.

144,000 Jewish converts will arise in the Tribulation and evangelize the world.

Post-Tribulation Rapture – Some believe the Church is removed at the end of the Tribulation. Other use the Pre-Wrath version which brings the Rapture back only a month or two from the end.

Therefore, if we have proven that none of the views are sufficient upon its individual merit due to the unanswerable statements within the Word, we are left with difficulty defining which one of the Rapture doctrines are sufficient. We may ignore the last book and others within the Bible altogether out of confusion and frustration. Disregarding the End Times is the direction that much of the Church has actually taken. They perceive themselves as Pan-Tribulationists, or that they believe that it will all pan out on its own without their own interpretative abilities plied to the topic. But, if 28% of Scripture deals with the End, it means that the subject is of significant relevance to God, and what He wishes to say to His children.

I have friends in ministry that tell me each time they bring up prophecy with those whom they have lost contact for a period of time, many evangelicals give the answer "I don't want to hear about what is going to happen in many years; I only want to know what God is doing today!" Many believe that understanding the complexities of prophecy are too ethereal, and therefore it is not a great use of their time. But, there is a better answer to this view.

As I stated earlier, II Timothy 3:16 indicates that "All Scripture is inspired by God and is profitable for teaching, for rebuking, for correcting, for training in righteousness." To take that deeper, the semantic is that each verse came from the lips of our Creator. We cannot skip a section, because we do not like where it is heading. Because something isn't understood well in life doesn't mean that one should ignore it!

I have, in my iPad, a Bible program called Olive Study Bible. This app allows me to take notes upon the Word and then organize them in folders. I have a folder called *Do Not Understand*. Those portions of Scripture have either completely or partially confounded me. I note the question mark, but then revisit them from time to time to see where my head is with God. Many times, He gives me one bit of wisdom that explodes in my mind with new perception that I didn't have before. We don't always understand all that we read in the Word at the moment it is taken in, but there is a time for everything under the sun, as Solomon wrote in Ecclesiastes.

When my friend, Jeff Swanson, would come over to watch the Denver Broncos each Sunday throughout each fall, we would pause the games, so that we could talk things we had learned over the years. We found out that both of us started studying the End Times from the same book by Hal Lindsey in the Summer of 1982. Each time we disagreed with one another, we agreed to not disagree and argue other teacher's positions (such as "Billy Joe Bob has this view"). We decided that we needed Scripture to explain itself. Our theories had to be based upon that firm foundation. Our divergences were solvable when based upon the whole Word of God. If one Scripture took a view out of position with our perception, then we needed to investigate it deeper or pitch the theory out, not the Word. Too many in the Church wish to dump the Word out first or use the trite comment, "I am not sure what that means, but I bet it doesn't mean what you think it says."

Again, give it some time and consider Godly counsel upon the Word. God would not have written it if He didn't see the verse as instructive to man's condition today or in the future. The next verse in order of II Timothy 3:17 completes the thought above "so that the man of God may be compete, equipped for every good work." Trust that the Lord will give you that insight into His ways, but do not allow the misunderstandings to divide us. Those who are Post-Trib Rapturists are just as strong of Believers in Christ as those who hold to the Pre-Trib view!

How about another analogy (most have to get used to my football analogies which are legendary among my employees)? My wife's parents paid for their daughter's college all the way through her graduate program out of their pockets without any loans. They wanted her to know that college was being funded for by them, and the reason why they paid for it was out of their love for her. If Wendy, at eighteen years old, would have come to her parents demanding an accounting of *how* college was to be paid, can you imagine the impertinence? Wendy's parents might have sat her down to demand a new level of guilt-laden respect. The fact was that they *had* written the checks for college, and it was a financial hardship to do so. God, in the same way, tells His children the *that's* and the *why's* related to prophecy, but not always the *how's*. If we knew the *how's* of the future, we may not trust Him for His fulfillment of Scripture to make His glory known "among the nations." Therefore, I am not supposed to know when I will die or how (I am hoping that I will go in the Rapture, though), because I need to be focused upon how I live this day. I am not promised tomorrow. But do you know that when God wrote each phrase in the Word, He wanted us to get the *Why's*? But often, it takes patience to discover the meaning.

Chapter 7

TAKING SCRIPTURE AT ITS WORD

In John 19:1, we learn that Jesus was flogged before His unjust execution. It was a severe beating, considering the evidence that the Shroud of Turin turned up, something of which I do believe is true after my own research. The other Gospels refer to His beating but never in the brutality such as Isaiah 52:14 prophesizes that Jesus was unrecognizable beyond understanding. Some even perceive that Jesus was weighed down with the sin of the world which could have changed his appearance as well. The condition that Jesus would have been in after His scourging indicated that His facial features could not be identified as recognizable to those around Him. Scripture is scant in its conversing upon the topic, but it is readily believed that Jesus was actually flogged. One reason that people do not disbelieve the text is that it is *not* controversial.

We mentioned earlier that "all Scripture is inspired by God..." meaning that if one verse supports a view about a particular topic then adherents of the Word, which is defined as Fundamental Christianity, have to give way to the voice of God inside of His truth. I know that there are many who do not believe that the Bible has to be fully true for the Faithful to believe in its main tenants. I find this utterly demeaning to God. It spits upon His own words as if they are not important.

Math professors at a university cannot suddenly decide *not* to teach Geometry, because they don't agree with the subject as a foundation of mathematics inside of the new concepts of math. Consequently, if I am allowed to take verses out of the Bible because they are inconvenient, where is the halting point? Who is to say that I pulled the correct verses out of Scripture? A folk tale repeated when I was in college was about a group of women decades ago who were thoroughly disgusted with William Shakespeare's sexual references within his plays. Though they were outraged by the instances of sex, these women understood that his foundational works needed to be studied in their school district. The problem with their annexation of his wording was that the truly sexual references were never really removed, because they misunderstood what they were reading.

Using the above logic that all Scripture must be included in the conversation of Eschatology, even if it is intolerable to certain groups of people who don't agree with a view, then we have a culmination to all that God wrote. Jeff Swanson and I agreed to debate about the Bible and not another's interpretation of End Time events starting with the three main Rapture concepts. What I realized in my observations of Scripture and other external research are that each verse has a place within the Bible. The exercise was an incredibly instructive discourse upon the groups of people to which the Bible refers. Specifically, how differently the Bible uses references to people groups that many apply only to the Church. Therefore, when we correlate the groups of people listed in the New Testament with the End Time conversations, we find a fascinating relationship with the two concepts.

Over and again, the Bible differentiates the groups of people based upon their belief and timeframe of their belief in God, not as a respecter of persons but in what they believe and when they come to that faith. Old Testament Saints, listed in Hebrews 11 that some call the *Hall of Faith*, all lived before the Messiah's first coming to the planet. Their faith intimated their blessing of eternal life with God, not what they did. King David is my favorite of this group.

David saw Bathsheba upon a rooftop and lusted after her, initiating his first sin within the story. Jesus mentioned in the Gospels that if one lusts after a woman, he had committed adultery in his heart. David's second sin was to bring her to his court and essentially force himself on her. The Bible doesn't directly assert a rape, but how could a woman of the time refuse the king? Then David conspired to have her husband killed to create the situation for Uriah's death. Nathan, after the conclusion of the sins, confronted David upon his many sins, and he then confessed and asked for God's forgiveness. Though David repented and is called a man after God's own heart (Acts 13:22), he will be resurrected in the beginning of the Millennial Reign along with the other Old Testament Saints because of the Blood of the Lamb. Eventually, King David will rule for a thousand years in Israel as the governor.

The process of forgiveness that David continued through his life provided a blueprint for restoring the follower of Christ to redeem one's relationship with his or her God. Confession doesn't change the fact that one has already been forgiven before "the Foundation of the Earth." This point is central to the understanding of the Cross of Jesus. Jesus already forgave us at the Cross, because He took our sins on. We don't need to re-crucify the Lord each time we sin, or beat ourselves in a perpetual rededication to our salvation so that we don't miss the Rapture. A friend of mine in ministry indicated that doctrines should of all types of Biblical knowledge should be filtered through the Cross of Christ. King David was modeling that behavior for all humanity.

John 20:24-29 tells of a story that was beautifully presented by a pastor I love to hear, Andrew Wommack in Woodland Park, Colorado. The Disciples and two of the women in the Upper Room had already seen Jesus in His bodily risen and believed in the impossible resurrection. They had been cloistered for eight days waiting for Jesus to give them their specific marching orders. It must have also been frustrating days trying to get their brother, Thomas, to believe that Jesus was actually *raised* from the dead.

Doubting Thomas staunchly claimed that he had to have physical proof of the wounds of his Master's body. After Jesus stepped through the portal of time within their hiding place, Thomas was instantly convinced by what he saw and needed no other proof. Jesus demanded that Thomas follow through with his unbelief by telling Thomas to put his hand in Jesus' side wound. Andrew Wommack indicated that Thomas gave the biggest evidence of faith anyone had done to that point and intimates that Thomas' proclamation "my Lord and my God" was a foreshadowing of the Church which will come into evidence within a few weeks of the events in John 20. With Thomas' confession, I believe that Pastor Wommack correctly identified the shadow beginning with the group I call Faithful, or the Church Age.

God always foreshadows important events in history. Those critical communications of changes were presented to the world as a testimony. Andrew Wommack shows that Thomas' statement was the first to proceed from lips of men that Jesus was God. The Disciples were always willing to indicate that Jesus was Lord over them, or their teacher/master;

but only Thomas indicated a new relationship with Jesus that soon the Church would take up the banner. It is the perfect anecdote of Hebrews 11:1 stating that "Faith is the evidence of things hoped for and the promise of things unseen." Jesus' response to Thomas was even more fascinating epitomizing that idea: "Because you have seen Me, you have believe. Those who believe without seeing are blessed." In this gripping pronouncement, I believe that our Lord was expressing the next group with which we may or may not be familiar called the Bride of Christ which I extend to using the analogy of the Faithful (handled in a later chapter).

Of course, this can be applied to life events or needs of the Church body to not succumb to the world, but it was also a comment, I believe, of the end of the Biblical story. We have three stories that the Scriptures indicate could occur in the Pre-Trib Rapture, Mid-Trib Rapture and the Pre-Wrath Rapture. But let me present the need for all Raptures, and the numerous conflicts depicted with each viewpoint as the only correct doctrine.

Rapture: Could There Be More than One?

Chapter 8

PRE-TRIBULATION RAPTURE ONLY

If the Church is the only group of people that leaves the world before Tribulation, then we have a problem with the Scriptures that strongly delineate potential Mid or Pre-Wrath Raptures. A singular view upon the Raptures suggests that we must remove all other precursors to the one view. It is a prevailing opinion, among prophecy teachers, that one of these above views are right, and the two others are wrong. For more than thirty years, I held to the Pre-Trib Rapture view only, but the Lord dealt with me. I didn't adjust my thinking based upon a "burning of the bosom" that motivated Joseph Smith in the 1800's to start the Mormon religion. This is a common critical error in which we believe that we can have a special revelation from God without the benefit of the Word backing the revelation. But the ideas, which I use the descriptor of *doctrine*, must fit within the breadth of the Word of God, not the other way around.

The continuance of one theory wasn't something I was interested in carrying the banner without the

Lord upon my shoulder to support it in the Word. In Revelation 7:9 it states the following: "After this I looked, and there was a vast multitude from every nation, tribe, people and language, which no one could number, standing before the throne and before the Lamb. They were robed in white and Palm branches in their hands." This is different in scope and discussion than other Pre-Tribulation Scriptures such as I Thessalonians 4:16-18 where we see the "dead in Christ" rising first then "we who are left" are gathered to Him. Let's investigate that further to explain the wording divergences of Revelation 7:9 versus Revelation 4:1 and others.

John explains in Revelation 4:1-5 that he is called up to the throne room (similar at the surface to the 1 Thess. 4:16-18 verses, of which I believe is a type and shadow of the Pre-Trib Rapture). It is a bodily transformation that he undergoes but doesn't explain at all. He then gives metaphor for a *Sea of Glass* with the innumerable ones who have come to acceptance of Christ before the Tribulation occurs. In Revelation chapters 4-5, Jesus will be standing upon the throne with the twenty-four elders arrayed about Him. I believe that this is a beautiful Heavenly snapshot of the throne of the Lamb with His Bride. The Pre-Trib Raptured are given their crowns who then cast those diadems at the feet of Him who is gloried throughout the Heavens.

John then weeps, because no one is found to be worthy to open the Seven Seals. The angel who sticks with him during his future vision chastises John indicating that only the Lamb can open the Seals. Then, Jesus introduces the Anti-Christ, in the First Seal, and the other three horsemen as well as the rest of the Seals. God seals a special group of young Jewish men who have never had sexual relations with women (Revelation 14 describes this intriguing group) from the twelve tribes of Israel which are called the

144,000. They will preach throughout the earth their message of the Kingdom which then leads to our above verse Revelation 7:9.

The Popular Handbook of the Rapture (2011, Tim LaHaye, Thomas Ice, and Ed Hinson) is a compilation of a very good study of Rapture verses. Dr. Ed Hinson in chapter 9 expounded on the controversy relating to the above verse. He stated that some prophecy teachers cannot explain why this verse shows that the 144,000 are no longer upon the earth along with people from every tribe and nation. Dr. Hinson believes that these people are martyred of Christ. The Seal, on the foreheads listed in chapter seven, gives clear indication that the witnesses cannot be harmed which makes the verse a conundrum for prophecy teachers.

So, let's back up and examine more of the 144,000 witnesses' path for a moment. If a witness cannot be killed because they are Sealed of God, how can they enter Heaven without dying? There are only two ways in which we leave this earth: one by death of the body and the other inside of a Rapture. One minute they are on the earth evangelizing in the largest amount of people that history has ever seen come to Christ and the next they disappear from the Revelation conversation. But to interpret Scripture correctly, one must read as many as ten to fifteen verses before and after to get an idea of its placement as well as the context of the verse, as the great Bob Yandian mentions in many of his own teachings.

Therefore, Revelation 7:9 is definitely centered with the people in Heaven, as a famous pastor Hilton Sutton indicates in Revelation Revealed published back in 1982. Dr. Sutton was one of the first prophecy teachers I am aware of who indicated that there might be more than one Rapture event. Very recently though, Perry Stone discussed three harvests of the believers written in Revelation indicating that the

144,000 Jewish men are also taken off the earth in a similar fashion as the Pre-Tribulation Church we discussed earlier.

A problem with the Pre-Trib Rapture position *only* is that the rest of the believers can only hope for two mechanisms for the Lord: martyrdom (of course it's nothing to hope for) or surviving until the Millennial Reign. Several verses in the New Testament have commented that we are *not* appointed to wrath (Romans 1:18, Rom. 2:5, and I Thess. 5:9). If that is true, how is it that only the ones who are in Christ before the Tribulation would be included in this group who goes to Heaven in Revelation 7:9? If those who believe in Christ are also not appointed to the wrath of God, how then can God not take them away from the wrath that is to come? This was the most problematic of my investigations of the Last Days. I used to relegate those Believers who were called later in Revelation, as the Tribulation Saints, to either martyrdom or wrath.

I struggled mightily with this concept for years. I would meet or read a teacher's account of his interpretation of the End. Many convincing arguments can be debated for these Rapture positions for one or another. The Pre-Trib notion was both my favorite, for the obvious escapism reasons that anyone could admit, and the one that is most prominent throughout the New Testament. The Old Testament does not contain any mention of the Rapture since the Church was not understood as a concept. But before we finish this idea, let's look at the next Rapture.

Chapter 9

MID-TRIBULATION RAPTURE ONLY

With a Mid-Tribulational Rapture, it would indicate that those who live through the beginning of the Tribulation will probably not experience much in the way of the wrath of God (again, in most prophecy teacher's analysis). I stated earlier that adherents to this viewpoint believe that the focus of the Tribulation is awaiting the Anti-Christ and then to be taken away somewhere in the middle of the Tribulation. I would say that this powerful man is the sideline to the story, when it comes to the destiny of Believers in Christ.

Why is the Anti-Christ the sideline? The focus of the Tribulation is the separating of those who will follow Jesus and those who choose against Him. Now, I will tell you that there is a part of me that would like to be here upon the earth to identify the Anti-Christ, and then shout from the rooftops about him who steps to the forefront of the scene! What a time of witnessing the people of the earth will have!

The biggest problem with the Mid-Trib point is the weight of the verses related to Matthew 24:43-44, which is right in line with the End Time teaching that

Jesus is telling His disciples: "but know this: if the homeowner had known what time the thief was coming, he would have stayed alert and not let his house be broken into. This is why you also must be ready, because the Son of Man is coming at an hour you do not expect." If the Rapture of the Church occurs at the middle of the Tribulation (this also goes for the end of the Tribulation viewpoint as well), then the Christians could calculate the number of days in which we would leave the earth.

Why? Once you rightly divine the signing of the Peace Treaty with Israel and the Anti-Christ in Daniel 9:27, it is an easy calculation to accomplish the task and all of the mystery of the above verses vanish. The Church would be standing on their rooftops just as many did after a silly book written called <u>88 Reasons Jesus Will Return in '88</u> (don't bother with this book). In that book, the writer spewed his 88 reasons that Jesus had to return in 1988. All of them were ultimately lies, because he wasn't hearing from the Lord. People sold all they had and were waiting upon the mountains of Colorado, where I lived at the time, when I saw the spiritual end of this tragic prophecy, wanting to see Jesus come back at Rosh Hashanah of that year.

Even those who know the Scriptures but wish to stay inside of their sin could do the same calculation of the days until they might be Raptured. The time when Jesus would return for His Bride, in the Mid-Trib only aspect, would be an absolute known quantity. There are plenty of other verses in the Gospels that reiterate this same unknown viewpoint, therefore it leans the interpretation towards having both a Pre- and Mid-Trib Rapture.

Probably one of the toughest concepts to argue is the introduction of the 144,000 Jews. Why would God need 144,000 Jews to preach throughout the world with the Church still on the planet and suddenly energized with prophecy being fulfilled before our eyes? There would be no need for the Jews proselyting the world if we were around to do so. Now, some argue that the 144,000 are only preaching to the Jews, which is opposite of the Revelation 7:9 message that indicates that those who receive their message and enter the Kingdom are from every nation. It cannot be argued both ways that the 144,000 are preaching only to the Jews when it is clear that those in Heaven are from all nations and languages.

One other problem with the idea that the 144,000 preach to the Jews only is that Scripture throughout the New Testament indicates that it is near the end of the Tribulation that the Jews will "look upon the One they have pierced" (John 19:37 points the time when Jesus dies on the Cross, which seems to fulfill an End Time prophecy). No, it cannot be *only* a Mid-Trib Rapture.

Chapter 10

POST-TRIBULATION RAPTURE ONLY

Post-Trib Rapture opponents claim that this concept could be referred to as the Great U-Turn. The Post-Trib idea has Believers surviving on the earth through the greatest cataclysms known to man and potentially dying for their faith. Those who endure by hiding out in the woods, so to say, may see Christ come back for them toward the end of the Tribulation only to return a little later on (whether that be a few days or a month later within the Pre-Wrath concept of the Post-Trib Rapture). Jesus steps back on the earth in Revelation 19:11: "Then I saw Heaven opened, and there was a white horse, its rider called Faithful and True, and he judges and makes war in righteousness." In this Post-Trib Rapture only position, Believers come back from Heaven very quickly.

The Post-Trib position also has significant problems when considering how it is perceived. We mentioned earlier that most have migrated to the Pre-Wrath mindset, so that around thirty days before the end of the Tribulation, the Believers/Church will be taken from the earth. In this perspective, the

Christians must suffer most of the severe torture that comes with the Seals and Trumpets, but possibly not the Bowl judgments. This view also never really deals with Believers as the Bride of Christ and what that means.

Jeff Swanson, the aforementioned creator of the Bible chronology www.PlanBible.com, indicates that the Seal, Trumpet and Bowl judgments are not as chronological as most would understand. First, Revelation feels, on the surface, to be a relatively step-by-step book through a future timeframe. Portions, to be sure, were referred to as chronological. It should also be noted that this incredible theological opinion of the timing of the 21 judgments are also held in the above estimation by Dr. Irwin Baxter who is also of the Pre-Wrath view for the Rapture.

The Sixth Seal, Seventh Trumpet, Seventh Bowl and the Third Woe are all hauntingly similar to one another. If we understand that the judgments are sequential as some classical research presents it, then in the first approximate two years of the seven-year timespan, we have such a massive earthquake that the celestial heavens will be out of place. With the Seventh Bowl, the earthquake has all the cities falling down and huge hailstones falling upon the people of the earth. If these are four separate events, then how can the earth even survive for a moment after a worldwide quake? The devastation would effectively kill off the whole world's ability to bring about the Mark of the Beast, not to mention war that will occur after the earthquake. They are so similar that Mr. Swanson and Dr. Baxter believe that they are the same event which would make more sense that the Seals are throughout the entire seven years; the Trumpets occur in the last half of the Tribulation; and the Bowls end the cataclysm within the last few months.

If the above is true that all of this judgment is a

massive earthquake that levels cities, mountains and all land masses at the same time, then there is no possible way for anyone to survive until the end. The judgments are significantly worse than one might image. I have spent years upon this topic, but now truly believe that these Seven Years are almost unimaginably worse than any person can possibly describe, but let's consider the survivalist's ability to subsist.

The Third Trumpet indicates that one third of the fresh water sources will be bitter due to a comet hitting the earth, and the Fourth indicates that the sun, moon and stars will be darkened by a third as well. No food? Barely any water? That would disrupt what you could do in an underground shelter if one of those were destroyed. All the hard work to accomplish one shelter would be for naught with water supplies buckling for the people. No, God doesn't ask us to survive the Tribulation. He asks His children to preach the Gospel in any time that they may be able.

Many of the same problems that plague the Mid-Trib position transfer over to the Pre-Wrath outlook as well. We mentioned the 144,000 Jews earlier that are preaching, but then are suddenly gone in the middle of the timeframe (Revelation 7:9). We can further note that the Two Witnesses show up on the scene in the second half of the Tribulation. Some erroneously have these Two preaching in the beginning which truly isn't needed with the 144,000 around to accomplish the evangelism of the world. The days of the Witnesses are numbered at three and a half years, so a prophecy teacher must utilize them in positioning to the first or the last half of the Tribulation. The Two Witnesses will preach that the world is headed for judgment, of which is exactly what happens in the second half of the Tribulation as the world is hurled into the toilet.

Revelation 14:6 indicates that an Angel of the Lord will join the Two Witnesses flitting about the earth to preach "the everlasting Gospel." We don't exactly know how the Witnesses and this Angel will extend the message to the world trying to correct unbeliever's perceptions. I find it fascinating that God only indicates that three will be teaching in this last time frame for the world. Some might see it as incongruous that only three personalities accomplish the final task of evangelizing the globe, but God has His own way of doing a deed (including the concept that the Trinity is all that is needed for God's completion of Himself).

During the 1940-1950's, tent revivals were effective in changing the hearts of men and women to Christ by communicating messages about the "fires of Hell." While this isn't a new concept to give to the world, the delivery was novel for the Traditional and Greatest Generations. Fear is a powerful motivator to create Soul change. The unfortunate side-effect is that if the fear cannot be sustained, then the message becomes watered down in the hearer. During the last three and a half years, the Gospel could potentially have this same type of ring to it. Hell will literally be played out for the world stage as Shakespeare bespoke in "As You Like It" by Jacques to Duke Senior. The players of this havoc will display the tragedy with their life's blood.

Doubling Back to the U-Turn

But probably the greatest problem with the Pre-Wrath, Post-Trib perspective as a single Rapture is the great U-turn. Why would Christ take His people off the earth to turn right around to bring them back to the planet in Revelation 17:14 where they come with Him to rule and reign during the 1000-year reign? What's the point? Why not just supernaturally protect or hide them in one such place as Petra where the last Remnant Jews (not the 144,000 preaching Jewish, young men) will be hidden? That would make ultimately more sense. This is never answered by the adherents of Pre-Wrath, Post-Trib view.

There is another flaw that is almost as damning to the position of the timing of the Pre-Wrath, Post-Trib Rapture only. If all the Christians leave approximately 30 days before Jesus sets up His reign (which literally is written in several portions of Scripture in the New and Old Testaments approximately 45 days after the end of the Tribulation as a transition to the Millennial Reign of Christ ruling upon the earth), then who is left upon the earth to populate the earth in the Millennium?

I had a gentleman who read some of my information. He then reported to me that he believed in a Post-Trib view of the Church. When I confronted the above issue of who might enter the Millennial Reign with Christ, he retorted that maybe "lesser bad people" might inhabit the earth with Jews during the 1000 years. When I asked him to explain further, he felt that Christ would preach to those unsaved people as well to convert them through the Millennium. This truly doesn't answer WHY we have a Tribulation then. If we can have a Tribulation in which non-Believers in Christ can somehow make it to the end of that seven years without accepting Christ, how do we explain Revelation 22:11 where it states, "let the unrighteous go on in unrighteousness"? How can we explain the separation of the Sheep and the Goats (Goats to Outer Darkness)? No, non-believers in Christ cannot inhabit the earth in the beginning of the Millennium.

Inside of the same Pre-Wrath position, there is also the above curious verse in Revelation 22:11. I had never been able to reconcile this unlikely Word. Why would God feel this way, letting the unrighteous go on in unrighteousness? Obviously, there are people who are incorrigible and will have already made up their minds about the Gospel. But the above position doesn't comment upon the few people groups left on the earth: the people left over are those who have taken the Mark of the Beast and are unredeemable or the Goats mentioned in Matthew 25. There is no one left after this short time of wrath which can enter the Kingdom if all believers have been removed from the planet!

If there are no potential Believers left upon the earth, then how can the Scriptures regarding the Millennial Reign of Christ occur with the two groups that it mentions: the Nations and the Remnant of Israel as in Zechariah 14:16-18 and other places? One of the last groups is the one third remnant of Jews which will be saved all at once and that survive until the Lord sets up His Reign upon the earth, and the other nations of people who must come up to Jerusalem each year to celebrate the feasts (sometimes referred to as the Nations). I believe that they are fulfilling one of the Fall Feasts of Israel needing to be completed by Christ in that they are celebrating the Feast of Tabernacles (The Feast of Trumpets and Yom Kippur I believe are fulfilled in the last ten days). The earth certainly cannot have non-Christians present at the time that Jesus steps upon the planet who will survive into the Millennial Reign, because they will be wiped off the earth with the False Prophet and the Anti-Christ, including the Goats whom we will next discuss. You must have a group of people who will believe in God after the wrath of God and before the Day of Wrath in which the earth is expunged from those who never believed in Him in the first place. Therefore, it makes no sense to have a final Rapture only as a position.

Chapter 11

THE INTRIGUING GROUPS OF PEOPLE IN THE END TIMES

To understand what is happening in Eschatology, I found that the *who* is much more important as well as the *why* and the *that*. Much as the analogy in the earlier chapter with my wife's parents paying for college, God wants us to know *who* is a part of *why* He is going to do. Sometimes, we don't know the *how* but are to simply trust.

As children of the living Father, He wants us to know about the events of the Last Days and the *whys*, but not always the *hows*. A child who demands the *how*, tends to reject the parent's gift and disrespects the sacrifice. God is not bothered with any sincere question that His children can ask, as I am not when my son has asked out of genuine curiosity. But the disrespectful questioning of my position and authority in relationship is one of the hardest lessons for a child and a parent to navigate effectively. This is also true with the Church to their Heavenly Father.

Too many times the Holy Spirit in Scripture

explains *that* a judgment is coming and *why*. We spend all our time trying to figure out *how* the future might come to pass and end up thinking ourselves as God by focusing on the wrong portion of the lesson or, at best, focusing upon the wrong lesson written in the Bible.

There are some prophecy teachers who spend their entire careers upon the realities of today. Folks, can I give you a hint? Nothing is happening in the world necessarily that needs to occur yet before Christ opens the First Seal and introduces the Anti-Christ other than the Rapture of His Bride (and maybe the Ezekiel 38-39 War of which we will mention a little later). Don't get bogged down trying to figure out what is happening in the Middle East. If we focus our vision upon the current possibilities, we miss what the Lord is really telling us: trust! Trust the One who has a purpose for your life. You have a job ahead of you; that job is to occupy (do business – whatever the Lord is directing you to accomplish). Concentrate on that!

I found that our focus was split when I started to realize that the Rapture speculations were all present and all probabilities, meaning that all the Rapture concepts were an amalgam. I saw the questions drip away and morph into the *who* was Raptured and *why,* and *when.* When I started to see, through the last six years (as opposed to the past 29 years of research) of studying the Scripture and endless research, the answers were staring me in the face: there were different groups of people to whom Jesus was referring within the Gospels.

Exclusionary Rapture Principles?

But understand me very clearly upon this topic, I am not trying to be exclusive, as some do on the *who* is to be Raptured or Saved. Jehovah's Witnesses and

Fundamental Mormon groups bring this exclusivity to their sects which are all based on unbiblical authority instead of being upon the Word of God. Jehovah's Witnesses believe that by 1935 (and that estimate changed several times throughout the 19th and early 20th centuries) all of the 144,000 American Jehovah's Witnesses were secure in their position of ruling with Christ during the Millennial Reign. The rest of them hoped that they would be resurrected and live upon the earth during the 1000-year reign. This cult is the ultimate replacement theology. Some Churches profusely believe that America has replaced the Jews as the Chosen people in God's heart. The answer is a resounding NO! John 15 tells us that we are grafted into the branch of God from the root of the Jews inside of God's planting of that vine. Jehovah Witness philosophies are based upon the flawed men's writings, not from a Biblical base, which shows the many untruths and changes over the years to accommodate those untruths.

The Fundamental Mormons (FLDS), who have split off from the Mormon Church (also unbiblical in nature), believe that they will be the only people that survive when God comes back to the earth again. They feel that they can be the only ones present when God recreates the earth, on which they will live in peace. The worldly will die the sinner's death in the judgments placed within the consequences of Revelation. They pick and choose their Scriptures to believe and fit them in how they want to believe. Of course, they have badly miscalculated, because they do not encompass all of the Bible into consideration. But, do you realize that much of the Church is skipping key Scriptures to prove their point about Eschatology as well?

A friend in ministry sat with a Pre-Wrath pastor at a Prophecy conference in 2016. The man told my friend that "God told me that only *we* are going to be saved at the end, (intimating that only a very few) and the rest will be pulverized." My friend shook his head knowing that what this man felt he heard from God wasn't what Scripture says about itself. Believe the Word over anything you might have heard. "Now, brothers, I have applied these things (*clever arguments that Paul was using*) to myself and Apollos for your benefit, so that you may learn from us the saying: 'Nothing beyond what is written." (1 Cor. 4:6 HCSB italics mine to explain earlier verses).

In 2018 I was rewriting this book, my wife and I stumbled upon a Saturday night movie on Amazon Prime called "Rapture" by Richard Lowry. Mr. Lowry had the Rapture event causing an electrical storm with cool cloud effects. He placed the Seven Thunders of Revelation 10 with powerful angels that were wiping out humanity in a vengeful indiscriminate fashion. Christians and non-Christians alike were being erased in a quick death out in the open like a lightening zap. God was mad and taking it out upon His creation. Only a precious few who inexplicably were playing an organ in a church (while the rest of the world had an Electro Magnetic Pulse stop all power) were safe, waiting for the Millennial Reign to begin. The Wrath was happening in one day without a seven-year period. Mr. Lowry pulled all kinds of Scriptures together as if they were spoken all at once in a flowing paragraph recited by a female actress. The problem was that half of the supposed references to the Word actually weren't in the Bible whatsoever!

Prophecy teachers must take special effort not to create logic leaps in their decision to explain future circumstances. So, if I predicted that the Pittsburgh Steelers might win the 2018 Super Bowl before that season, you may or may not agree with my prediction based upon some of the evidence I could present about their abilities to win it all. But if I predicted that the Vancouver Jackals will take the Super Bowl in

2018, any NFL fan would shake their head at me for not understanding the 32 teams that exist inside the league (if you know nothing of football, there are no Canadian teams).

When Jeff Swanson and I were finishing our series called ForeTold: Book One and Two, we took so few precious licenses making sure that we kept the Word intact, so that it wasn't violated despite it being fiction. The Church sometimes listens to these popular responses to the End Times with baited breath, including the fallacy that the start of the Tribulation by the Rapture of the Church was to be on September 23, 2017. The date seemed to refer to stars and planets lining up in Heaven such as Revelation 12 was intimating. The problem with this silly view was that by the time the point of Revelation 12 comes (which talks of a wholistic historical perspective of Satan from his beginning to when he is kicked out of Heaven), Satan is removed from the Throne Room of Christ with "great wrath knowing that his time is short." That is a direct response indicating the Middle of the Tribulation. It could not have occurred without many prophecies already being fulfilled. Don't be fooled until we take all prophecies together.

Go along with a spiritual journey my wife and I had as we were trying to get pregnant. We went to fertility specialists and were on our last round of fertility medications and artificial insemination (a somewhat humiliating medical procedure). The very last checkup told us that only one egg was viable, but that one was our son who is now in college in 2018. When we could compare the physiological changes within Wendy before pregnancy, they do not relate enough to after pregnancy is confirmed. Gestation creates a timeclock of biological changes in the woman's body (sorry women, we men are clueless during the whole process). Matthew 24:8 is when Jesus is discoursing the End Times from a Jewish perspective, because the

Disciples were asking the questions (always very important to identify who is talking and to whom is He is talking). Jesus stated "All of these events are the beginning of birth pains." This is a critical analogy that Christ sets up for His Bride. It is not a willy nilly comparison that we should not consider. There will be bad things in the Middle East and the world, for that matter. None of those should be our prophecy focus, because the timeclock (Daniel's clock of seven years) does not begin until the Anti-Christ signs his peace treaty with Israel. Jesus spiritually introduces him in the First Seal.

Birth pangs start a process of little biological changes, then rapidly becomes more dramatic as the second and the third trimester progresses for the mother and the baby. The End Times will be similar to that perceptive metaphor that Jesus presented. But let's step back a moment to see the groups of people with whom the New Testament is referring when it comes to Eschatology.

Chapter 12

THE FRIENDS

Many croon wonderful songs such as *What a Friend We Have in Jesus.* Darrell Evans (a creative worship leader that started in the mid-1990's in Tulsa) sang another beautiful one called *Favorite Friend* from the album *Let the River Flow* from 1997. These expound upon the friendship that we have with Jesus. While I would not try to dissuade the Church that Jesus can be your friend, we need to understand to whom He was speaking inside of John 15:15, "I do not call you slaves anymore, because a slave doesn't know what his master is doing. I have called you friends, because I have made known to you everything I have heard from my Father."

What this verse was telling the reader isn't as germane to this topic as about *whom* it was written. Most prophecy expositors don't think as I think; I may be somewhat different in the way I look at Scripture. Each time I consider what is written from the origin of the Bible in its absolute truth. All doctrine must conform to Scripture and not the other way around, including mine. One thing that I have learned is that we must ask to whom the writer is referring as well as whom the audience is. God knew His audience when He wrote the sixty-six books with the hands of the forty authors. The Lord was able to weave them together with a coherency that no other book has ever accomplished. He knew that mostly Christians and Jews would be reading the Scriptures.

Of course, others do read it, but they don't understand it fully. I was downgraded on a term paper in college by an English professor who didn't know that the Bible had different translations other than the King James Version (something that all English professors readily teach and should know because of the wide use of the Bible as literature throughout history until I corrected the error in her mind). Most other philosophers, who don't believe in the Bible, liberally quote from Scripture, even though they don't take much stock in its full content; the book is only used to prove their feeble points.

I had a friend more than twenty-seven years ago who told me that he read the Bible from cover to cover before he was a Christian. In my youthful admiration of him, I told him how cool I thought that was. He told me that it was the dumbest thing he ever did. He didn't understand what he was reading, because the Holy Spirit wasn't inside of him. It made little sense to me at the time. I would later understand that this made a world of sense. God knew that the primary readers would be Believers, so it had to be instructive for us as to His nature and what is important to Him. With the Holy Spirit inside us, we CAN understand it as we probe deeper.

The above passage of John 15:15 is referring directly to the Disciples and their relationship to Jesus. They graduated from Servants, who didn't know their master's bidding, into the role of being *Friends* with Jesus. Why are they the *Friends,* and we Christians who live today are not? Part of the definition of *Friends* is that a friend has face to face contact with others in any timeframe or era. The Disciples heard His voice and were the writers of the Gospels which was a special relationship to the Son.

Another potential example of a *Friend* would be the Old Testament writers who <u>knew</u> God and were telling the people of Israel, and the Bride, who God was. They were giving us revelation as to the Groom's nature as well as the Father (read Luke 12).

In Jewish tradition, the friends of the groom about to be married would blow trumpets and sound the alarm that the groom was coming into the city to take his bride to be with him into marriage. Isn't that exactly what we are waiting for Jesus to do for us (read Ephesians 5)? These Friends were the writers from the lips of God, and the transmission of all that we understand about the Son's time upon earth as well as what He accomplished through His death and resurrection. They had a terribly important work and one that is highly esteemed by the Father in Heaven. It is my opinion that they are also those referred to in Revelation 4, as they are a part of the 24 elders (which I think is a representation of both Old and New Testament writers) who are seated upon the throne beside Jesus.

But let me pitch something even more deep about the Old Testament giving veiled references to the New Testament understandings of the three Raptures. Enoch walked with God upon the earth and then he was no more (Genesis 5:24). He is referred to in many places throughout the Bible. Enoch's own writings have been retranslated by Jeff Swanson's Ministry and can found on his website (www.PlanBible.com). I believe that Enoch is the first translation into Heaven without death, as most theologians also believe, and a shadow of the First Rapture of the Faithful. He is very similar to the Friend of God in many ways.

Elijah, spoken of in the Old Testament and having a long book of his own, was a character who told it like it was without pulling punches. This was the same type of personality who I also believe comes as the second of the Two Witnesses. Elijah was taken up in a chariot in front of Elisha who received a double portion blessing of the Spirit that Elijah had (2 Kings 2:9). Enoch and Elijah are perfect possibilities of the Two Witnesses (of course we can only guess who they may actually be) as they did not experience physical death.

The last one taken up is much more public, which was Jesus Himself. Many saw Him after He died and was resurrected. Would Jesus be considered the last type of *Rapture*, similar to the a Pre-Wrath Rapture? I believe that this conclusion is absolutely possible and fascinating to ponder. All of these men were translated from their physical forms to a new altered state of Heavenly existence without the referent of death were eerily alike the Raptures described all over the New Testament.

Therefore, the writers of the New and Old Testaments, as well as the Disciples who didn't write anything in the Book, were a type of Friend who points us to the Father and His characteristics. Jesus stated within the Gospels that He only does what He sees His Father in heaven do. He was indicating the Father's will in all things and gave us a definite example to follow.

Chapter 13

BRIDE OF CHRIST: *THE FAITHFUL*

Friends – The Gospel and Old Testament Writers along with the Disciples who knew their Lord.

As a heterosexual man, I have never been terribly comfortable with the idea that I am the Bride of Christ, as other men have expressed this same struggle with this unique relationship with the Son. I love being the groom to my wife of more than twenty-five years as I write this. Women, on the other hand, do not normally have as much difficulty with this concept. But men and women *are* both co-heirs and the Bride of Christ. We are the ones written about in John 20:24-29, as we discussed earlier, when Thomas heard from Jesus: "Blessed are those who haven't seen me yet believe." What in the world does that mean?

There are many references to the Bride of Christ as in Ephesians 5. One of the more interesting verses is from John 3:29, "He who has the bride is the groom. But the groom's friend, who stands by and listens for him, rejoices greatly at the groom's voice. So, this joy of mine is complete." Here we have John the Baptist referring to himself as the friend of the groom. The friend of the groom announces when the groom is to come, but the Bride must be adorned for her husband to be (Rev. 21:2). What does that mean that the Church is the Bride, and that she must be adorned for Him?

Revelation 19:7-8 shows that John (the Disciple who is talking about himself) will be rejoicing and giving Jesus glory. The marriage of the Lamb will come at that point in Revelation 19, and the Bride must wear her wedding clothes. How can a Bride show up to a wedding without her clothes? Of course, she never does. The wedding clothes are the direct above metaphor of the righteousness of Christ. The books of Romans and Revelation explain the connotation of righteous acts, but that it is only seen with the Faithful in Heaven where she is presented. Can I digress a little bit here?

Do we get to have Wedding clothes by what we do? The answer is plainly NO! Isaiah 64:6 states "All of us have become like one who is unclean, and all our righteous acts are like filthy rags; we all shrivel up like a leaf and like the wind, our sins sweep us away." What in the world does this refer? Anything that we think that we can do for Christ is nothing in the grand scheme of things. It is by Grace that we are saved (Ephesians 2:8-9) and not by our works.

Here is an example. If I had a billion dollars and picked 1000 people to give one million to each, would the world see that as a good work (think of the old movie "Brewster's Millions" with Richard Pryor and John Candy)? The world would hail me as a saint. But if I did that, could I potentially do more harm than good for many people? YES! Do a Google search on those who have won the lottery, and you will find horror stories how instant wealth has made them poorer in the long run than healthy and happy. Giving money away could be deemed a good work in Christ. In the Spirit of Jesus, we must see that true good works need to be inside of what He tells you to do. Be in communication with God to know what He wants you to do, and you operate in wisdom that the Bible teaches. This is your occupation upon the earth as the Bride before your Groom comes!

But back on topic, the Wedding of the Lamb occurs sometime after the Bema Seat Judgment where her acts have been judged, during which I believe is at the timeframe of the Middle of the Tribulation (we will talk about the crowns a little later as well as the Bema Seat Judgment versus the White Throne judgment). This garment, referred to back in Revelation 19:7-8, will be worn by the Church who has sought His coming fervently and believed in the face of the world's disbelief in Jesus as our righteousness.

2 Peter 3:3-4 tells us "First, be aware of this: scoffers will come in the last days to scoff, living according to their desires, saying, 'Where is the promise of His coming? Ever since the fathers fell asleep, all things continue as they have been since the beginning of creation.'" These sentences tie together the beginning of Scripture to the end of all the days upon the planet inside of two verses. Peter utilized an intriguing word: in the Greek, *Scoffer* means *False Teacher*. Does that not alter the context of what Peter is trying to say? *Scoffers* have always been *False Teachers* who didn't believe in Jesus' return. The New Testament asks us to hold firm to the belief that He is returning to the planet in visible and physical form. But first, Jesus comes for the Bride.

The Faithful believe all the Bible is true, and some call us Fundamentalists for this certainty. I am glad to be including in this group. Over and again, the Bible has been proven both historically true and futuristic in its explanations. Satellite images likely will send the signal around the earth as in Revelation

11:7-10 (especially in verse nine which states that the Two Witnesses in death will be seen by the world as in "nations will view their bodies"), so that the whole world will look upon the slain Two Witnesses for three and one-half days. These were preposterous messages within Scripture as little as seventy years ago, but now they are a commonplace possibility with the invention of satellite TV.

The message of the New and Old Testaments have survived and have more documentation than the works of Shakespeare who wrote his plays from 1590-1610. Why does a significant portion of the body of Christ not believe in its writing? My personal question to those is simple: if you don't believe it, then why practice the faith? The simple response is that we have False Teachers among us who do not teach the message that the Father has given us inside of the Word. Revelation 1:3 shows that when we pay attention, keep His prophecy intact and understand by studying the message within the book that there is a special blessing.

Later, I will deal with the Wedding Feast and the Marriage of the Lamb that cements the relationship with Christ that the Church Age (up until the Rapture of the Church) has with her Lord. I personally love the passage of Hebrews 11:1 I have quoted before in, "Faith is the evidence of things hoped for and the promise of things unseen." This verse has sustained my Soul through dark times in which I thought my business was going to fail. There were other trials in which the world was telling me the opposite of what my faith was indicating through my Spirit which is seated in Heavenly places (Eph. 2:6). Faith is the only currency by which the Bride exchanges with the Son of God to procure the blessing of the Pre-Tribulation Rapture. Financial systems in governments require an agreed upon currency by which the buyer and seller can translate their goods and wealth to one another. God only deals in *faith* when He receives anything from humanity. The Lord pays out that *faith* in His abundant promises for His people who believe for their needs.

When we today consider Hebrews 11:1, we envision *evidence* as a legal hearing to indicate to the judge that what might have occurred in a case was true, specifically that a crime had been committed even though there might not have been a witness of one who saw the crime. The *promise* is a surety that our Souls and Spirits have a promise given. Another way to see this verse comes if you consider that I could inherit a large portfolio of funds. The promise would be the legal paperwork in which my name is written along with the amount of the inheritance. The evidence is the amount in the bank accounts that what is promised can be delivered as well as the assurance that it is legal in the state in which one resides. That's what the Church must hold on to with all of her soulish might. Faith actually is the key component of the Faithful.

Lastly, we need to explain a teaching that is passing among the churches. The sum of the idea is that the church needs to get back to its roots and that it is not faithful. There is a portion of that concept which is valid. We do need to return to the roots of the Word. That does prove us to be Faithful to the Lord in our showing that we are waiting for God to show Himself among the nations. But saying that the Church/Bride needs to complete a work, which is somewhat innate inside of this overall teaching, is the falsity of the preaching. The Church isn't faithful based upon what they do in their walk of trying to be pure. They are faithful in that Christ said they were. Their belief in Jesus as the Faithful One gives us entrance inside of His righteousness which makes us Faithful. My son cannot do anything to remove his sonship in my house. He will always have that position. We do as well in Christ.

Therefore, I propose a radical thought that I have been employing for the past year. The next time you catch yourself in that sin or shortly thereafter, tell the Devil this statement: "Yeah I did that. But I am Faithful Satan. Get out." I know at that moment you committed that sin that you don't *feel* Faithful, but it's not a state of being. It is a position of the character of Christ that was instilled from the Cross to you based upon your belief in Him. Trust me, Satan has to flee from that message. What's he gonna say? Only his base message is to lie that you are not acting faithful. God doesn't need you to act faithful to show that you already have that inside the crown upon your head in the Spirit realm. Just put the Flesh in the grave where is it supposed to lie, along with Satan's lies.

Chapter 14

THE CHOSEN AND THE 144,000 JEWS: THE BEGINNING OF THE TRIBULATION

Friends – The Gospel and Old Testament Writers along with the Disciples who knew their Lord.

Faithful/Bride – the Church is the Bride of Christ and the Faithful of Christ.

Of these next two groups of people (Chosen and 144,000), we will first turn our attention to the Chosen gentiles. Neither of these groups exist today as a definable set of people in the Lord, because the conditions for them to collate aren't ready. One of the best and most difficult verses for most prophecy teachers to explain about the Chosen is the following in Luke 12:48: "But those who did not know and did things deserving of blows will be beaten lightly..."

Prophecy teachers indicate that the Tribulation Saints (those born-again after the Pre-Tribulation Rapture of the Church) will be characteristic of the Church, or maybe even Faithful Believers at one time who have fallen away from Christ, or even one who really wasn't with Christ at all. The Chosen are to be referred to in Matthew 24:22 indicated as the Elect as well.

Those who did not know

Luke 12:48 starts out with an interesting phrase of "those who did not know." I believe that this means they didn't know anything of the coming of the Lord. Why? Reading the context of Luke 12, another one of my favorite chapters, indicates that it explains with how Christ will deal with Believers. Some mistakenly perceive that Christ is going to beat His Church up a bit. If He were to do this type of scourging of the Bride of Christ, as some would purport, then it denigrates to Cross He paid for all of humanity! Why does Jesus need to beat His people for their sins? He already took it all upon Himself. So it is therefore not indicating a judgment beating that Christ will do!

These people simply do not know about the coming of Christ. They have spent no time understanding what God was talking about in His coming. I will give you a little fictional account later in this long chapter to explain. They were ignorant.

They Did Things Deserving of Blows will Be Beaten Lightly

Herein lies the primary confusion that needs context as to what Jesus is explaining. In the whole chapter of Luke 12, He is talking about different groups of people. All are slaves to Christ. That is innate in the teaching, other than those who are willfully against Him (of whom are the Goats that will be detailed later on). I believe that they did things deserving of blows actually means that they were not in compliance with the confession of Christ so they were taking the sin upon themselves instead of upon Christ's back. Every unbeliever obtains this level of silly choice, of course their own choice inside of Free Will, to accept the punishment of sin.

But the only punishment of sin is death. We can't be beaten to accomplish the extraction of sin out of our lives or we sully the nature of the Cross and what Jesus did. If they are slaves to Christ, they are Believers later on! It is my assertion that the Chosen will exist in a time of complete turmoil and as a result of their choice NOT to believe when they could have escaped with the Faithful in the Pre-Trib Rapture, they will then suffer the consequences of the time of Jacob's trouble which is the Tribulation.

They are beaten a little, because the world hates them. This is a part of their future testimony in Christ that will define them as a group. Chinese Christians today are absolutely living this type of torture for their faith. These future Christians will also have to endure it, not because they did anything bad. They will endure the beatings of the world because of the time in which they survive: the beginning of the seven year Tribulation.

Revelation 17:14 Wording of the Chosen

The Chosen does not exist in the minds of most Bible teachers, because it is my belief that they haven't even seen them within Scripture. We must understand, as stated earlier, that there are three distinct groups in which the Word is intimating. Revelation 17:14 "These will make war against the Lamb, but the Lamb will conquer them, because He is the Lord of lords and King of kings. Those with Him are the *called, chosen,* and *faithful.*" It is such a curious statement that most prophecy teachers skim through, because John is making a unique statement as to those who are coming with Jesus. I agree that the focus is upon Jesus when the throngs of Heaven enter the arena of the earth in this supernatural form. But it is my studied approach that Christ is revealing another layer of the onion which is Scripture. Just from a writing perspective, no expositor, who believes that Revelation 17:14 are just the Bride or Christians today, has ever really detailed why John used separate Greek words to explain those behind Jesus on their horses.

The Jews have long held the belief about the Bible that there are layers of interpretation upon more layers. It is why any serious student of the Word can find him or herself stuck on a verse for days and weeks, receiving deeper meaning of the sentences within. I respond to the Word by choosing not to gloss over statements in it and digging at the meaning of each word within the context of the verse within the context of the chapter (you must understand that chapters and verses didn't exist when they were written, but the context might be outside of the arbitrary verses and chapters given).

Revelation 17:14 indicates that there are three groups of people who will be coming with Christ to take the earth back for the Kingdom. The people with Christ will do little in the transformation of the planet, because Jesus will accomplish it and does, before the foundation of the world, by His Word. Most believe that these words are descriptors of the Bride, but that's not God's style in writing. He is always trying to make a point in the Word. The words are Called (*Kletos* which means to be appointed as a saint or *Hagios*), Chosen (*Eklektos* which means Chosen or Elect of Christ or even picked out by God) and Faithful

(*Pistis* which is trustworthy faithful believer in Christ). Faithful is the exact wording Jesus uses in the description of the Church who in John 20:27 when He declares to Doubting Thomas that there will be a group of people who believe without seeing. While we will discuss the Called later, let us deal with the Chosen as I have found them in the New Testament.

Chosen and How They must bear Deception

In Matthew 24:24 it states that "False messiahs...will arise to perform great signs...to lead astray, if possible, even the elect." Most Prophecy teachers see that there will be a great deception after the beginning of the Tribulation; it does not matter if you believe in a Pre-Trib or Post-Trib Rapture. Prophecy teachers agree that the Saints (*Hagios*) will be lacking in their understanding of the Scriptures, of which I heartily agree.

Consider that a new Saint has barely had time to contemplate the nature of those lost in the first Rapture giving him a dizzying amount to process including grief and loss all about him. The verses around Matthew 24 do not state that *Hagios*/Saints will be changed from their conviction of Christ as their Savior, but that it will be a powerful story to potentially sway or influence them. When one is in grief (read online about the Stages of Grief for more information) such as those who are waylaid by the consequences of millions of people missing from the planet, decisions about their next steps will be difficult to make. It is easy for the grieved person to make poor choices upon his or her future which creates the reprehensible behavior of some who prey upon their weak period of time to sell something to the grieved. In this future instance, millions will be dealing with their grief all at once.

Romans 8:29 and 33 uses the same word of Chosen but adds in the concept that they were "predestined" and "foreknown." This wording is another interesting tidbit of the Chosen's nature. While many believe that this is a direct tie to the Church, and I think we can agree that today's Christians learn from this information that Paul shared with us, I believe that Paul was referring to a group of people who would need special help upon a day of trouble inside the clever words that only the Holy Spirit could know.

While Romans is not a book that spends much direct references upon Eschatology, it obliquely denotes to the Last Days throughout the book. The Church over the centuries has argued about Predestination and Free Will ad infinitum, but we have put that to rest inside of the book of Romans relatively clearly beforehand. All have Free Will to choose but when we choose Christ, He stated clearly that He has a destiny for those who live inside of His Will. But will the people of the Tribulation need a more constricted road (not to limit their actions) to protect them from the harm to come? That is absolutely clear throughout all readings of the Believers in the times to come. All will die if Christ delays one day longer to step onto the planet (Matt. 24:22).

Did you realize that the God of the Universe has made a plan to see the Chosen, before the foundation of the world, to be believers in Christ during the first part of the Tribulation? I believe that these people are Elected by God because of the choice they make in Christ during the beginning of the most turbulent time in humanity's history. I am distinguishing that God has a plan for those people to keep them from perishing too early. Why? Every time I study Eschatology anew, I find that the End Time is more perilous than the last time I searched the Scriptures. It cannot be underestimated in the death toll be it in the beginning of the Tribulation or in the last half called the Great Tribulation. God has a plan for those who come to Christ with more grace than He has exhibited in the past. In a time in which Sin will abound even higher than has ever been realized, "grace will be multiplied even more..." Romans 5:20.

Great Times of Trouble Change the World

The Elect/Chosen will be the people group who come to a saving knowledge of Jesus after the Faithful, Pre-Trib Rapture of the Church are gone. They will experience the earth after millions of Christians exit this physical existence. Barna (a strong Christian-based research group) indicates that as many as 9-10% of the world are Christians in the true sense of the word. This means that they believe in the Bible and have faith in Jesus as their personal Lord and Savior (Romans 10:9-10). If we make it easy for the math challenged like me, that would mean that there are approximately 800 million Christians worldwide or 35 million American Christians missing from the planet, considering the world population is approximately eight billion and America has 350 million citizens.

Consider this: World War I historical estimates are that 30 million individuals were casualties of the Great War. The maps of Europe were permanently altered, changing from larger kingdoms to more specific nation states. The America that existed after the Great War, who was already somewhat isolated (before that war) and the WWI generation still able to taste war from their own youth, was loathed to enter the fight in the 1939-1941 timeframe in which Hitler was spoiling for his own fight.

Franklin Delano Roosevelt, FDR, knew that we would have to come to the aid of Europe and the Pacific sooner than later. The USSR was on the edge of collapse in the early 1940's, while England was hanging on by a bloody thread. WWII took more than 70 million, including six million Jews and five million other undesirables from Europe alone by the Nazi regime purging whole civilizations. Again, the maps were adjusted for the breakup of nations and people groups who wanted to live together created a new self-determination. The later 40's through the 60's experienced an even greater fragmentation in ethnic groups dividing themselves with severe revolutions killing untold new regimes and people. America, on the other hand, lost 365,000 men and women in WWII. Casualty figures were as high as 625,000 during the Civil War killing as many as one percent of the American population (I am not belittling the sacrifice but putting it within the world perspective of deaths during World War II mind you). But consider this: when thirty-five million Christian Americans leave in a sudden, fantastic fashion with the Pre-Trib Rapture, it will be categorically unimaginable, not to mention the 800 million Christians disappearing worldwide.

Trucking would literally be shut down and services, such as basic as electricity and trash collection, could almost cease to exist for a significant time. Some who believe in a Post-Trib or a Mid-Trib Rapture perceive that the beginning half of the Tribulation will not be bloody or turbulent as opposed to the second half of the Tribulation. This is not correct. Matthew 24, from Jesus' own mouth, indicates that as a mother's time is drawing near to delivery, the signs by her contractions become more frequent and intense. That analogy can be applied to the American Economy which will effectively spring a huge, collective leak.

When the 9/11 tragedy jolted all of us with the 3000 Americans dead in the heart of the of our financial sector as well as in Washington and Pennsylvania, the Stock Market crashed. I know of five hearing aid businesses that can point to their downfall from that one day. Think of the financial chaos when hundreds of millions are missing. My Audiology office will be closed in a day, never to reopen. Inflation and jobless claims, without the ability of the government to completely step in, will only be rivaled by banks failing, because the FDIC (Federal Bank Deposit Insurance) will not be able to cover the run on the banks as people run to ATM's without ability to extract their cash, not to mention credit cards seizing at the wrong time. This will be the economic condition in which the people of the world will require a leader to step in to calm the raging economic storms worldwide.

What Gog Does to the World of the Tribulation

I also believe that the Gog and Magog War must blow up in a multi-nation conflict, albeit a short one, before the beginning of the Tribulation. The Anti-Christ would then step in as the Ezekiel 38-39 war ends with a world into a hot mess. Possibly millions of soldiers from as far north as Russia to southern European countries, not to mention other mostly Islamic armies, will flood into eastern Israel to take peace from her land. All the while, several countries (Ez. 38:13) will "watch from afar," potentially Britain and America, who will tell Gog that they despise the looting actions of the invading nations. The text suggests that those republics will do nothing to impede the unfolding drama in the Middle East in this huge future war before the Tribulation.

Three main events will set the Magog armies (the above coalition armies under a Russian army and a leader known as Gog) ablaze in quick succession. First, a localized earthquake will occur that will be powerful but small enough in eastern Israel just after they begin to threaten Israel in their swift attack.

Second, there will be a perceived super weapon that the Israelis will employ against the armies to confuse them. Scripture points that God will operate this weapon against the invaders, though (and your guess is as good as mine as to what this weapon is and what calamity it brings). The armies will then begin to fight against one another as Gog, the human leader of this huge band of military forces, will witness the killing of his own men.

Third, I believe a tactical nuclear weapon or a chemical weapon will kill off the rest of the attackers. The first sign with regards to the earthquake might be considered just bad luck timing that always accompanies an attack. All military leaders know that "acts of God" can plague the battlefields of their plans with unforeseen consequences. But the third occurrence, which might be anticipated by Gog as Israel's nuclear deterrent to gain the upper hand in any battle, will startle the troops with the lasting effect. Scripture says that the *confusion attack* will be considered a weapon by the rest of the world leaving them quaking in their boots, not believing their lack of intelligence agencies about the effects of this weapon. I believe that when the world sees first hand this potential confusion weapon employed by the Jews, they will be forced to sue for peace. But it will already be too late for the opponents of the God of Israel. She does not normally negotiate with those who harm her; she always makes those pay for their transgressions. This invasion will be the pinnacle of the wars against her since her rebirth in May of 1948. From 1948 until that day, many bloody invasions have been come to crush the Israelis into dust. Each time the reprisal is swift and deadly.

The World has their New Leader

It is possible that the Anti-Christ will be able to rush in to create a peace when no other leader in history has ever been able to complete. For any American leader at any time, an armistice in the Middle East would be considered a virtual feather in the cap of the negotiator who took credit for it. This world leader, (the Anti-Christ) who rises from obscurity (Revelation 13:11-14), will be able to achieve that which no one will believe is possible. But it can only happen after the Faithful group, which is also called the Bride, is taken out of the way. II Thessalonians 2:7-8 indicates that the Holy Spirit within the Believer must be gone for a timeframe to introduce the coming "man of lawlessness." The Elect or the Chosen will have inherited, by their inaction with Christ in their hearts, a world gone mad. Little will help them make sense of what they watch on the news, other than the introduction of the crafty group called the 144,000.

Now reverting to the after events of the Rapture of the Bride, in Revelation 4 and 6, we read that John is weeping in Heaven, because no one, above or under the earth, is found worthy to open the Seals. An angel chides John, explaining that the Lamb of God is able to complete the task that no other creature can. Jesus then steps in to introduce the Anti-Christ in the First Seal. Some erroneously think that this First Seal is Jesus, which is preposterous. Imagine the wording in Revelation 6:2 states "I looked, and there was a white horse. The horseman on it had a bow: a crown was given to him, and he went out as a victor to conquer." When does Jesus ever need a bow without arrows to conquer? To have a bow without arrows means that he could wield some military might, but he will not for some reason which leads most prophecy teachers to believe that he does he work through diplomacy. But his brand of diplomacy will be heavy handed. How can anyone believe that he is given a crown for the one who is called King of all kings? This is obviously the Anti-Christ in every sense of the word.

We mentioned earlier that the biggest problem with a Mid-Trib Rapture is that the Faithful would be screaming bloody murder at a leader who purports any of the roles that the Anti-Christ will do. But if the Pre-Tribulation Believers are missing, few with any knowledge are available to expose the truth of his real identity.

The After-Effects of a Pre-Trib Rapture

The above is one of the strongest points of a Pre-Trib Rapture and backed up by Scripture in II Thessalonians 2:3 (take note of the signature words of deception innate in the Word): "Don't let anyone deceive you in any way. For that day will not come unless the apostasy comes first, and the man of lawlessness is revealed, the son of destruction." Much conversation in prophecy circles center around the word *Apostacy*. Some believe that this occurred (a falling away from truth) when the Muslims began their changing of the Gospels and the Jewish Torah in the seventh century AD. Others feel that it will be inherent in those before the Rapture of the Church, or today seeding the point that we are moving away from the lips of God guiding our lives. I somewhat agree with those views, but they are not primary to what I wish you to consider. Paul tells the reader to not be deceived and that there has to be a falling away before the Anti-Christ comes upon the scene. There are other teachers, such as Pastor Bob Yandian, who actually take a more interesting approach on this topic stating that the *Apostacy* is the Rapture of the Bride. The worldly description that will be enacted by the media will probably be another way of indicating how a deception will arise while the Anti-Christ tries to explain away a spiritual occurrence of those who have left this earth without a trace.

There will be men and women who are suddenly without their children on the earth and crying for their missing loved ones. It is my belief that those who are under the age of accountability (whatever age that a child understands their sin and their response to it) will be Raptured in that first exit of the Faithful. There are some who are left behind will instantly recognize what is happening in the world. It might be hauntingly like the character Rayford Steele in the wildly popular book that started in the 1990's, and ended with its twelfth book in the mid 2000's, *Left Behind's* first book. Rayford, the main character and a pilot, moves quickly to a saving knowledge of Jesus as well as his Pastor, left behind Bruce Barnes, who realizes his own hypocrisy not believing in Jesus when he could have been Raptured. It is a wonderful story of salvation during a confusing time trying to separate one from reason. Beginning Believers in that future time will have little knowledge of the truth, and potentially are just trying to figure out their own place within the New World Order. Most people don't know what the Rapture means just as similarly as the word Apocalypse. The prevailing semantic of the word Apocalypse to most Americans is the destruction of the world in a great cataclysmic event, but what it really means is an unveiling. That limited knowledge will certainly infect those surviving the Pre-Trib Rapture.

Evangelizing Jews Numbering 144,000

The Jewish men in the *Left Behind* series were instantly converted into the conceptual tribe of the

144,000 protected Jews, but the men themselves were not perfect representations of what the Bible states about this group. They will be young, virgin men (Revelation 14) who are inspired by God to come to a saving knowledge in Christ Jesus. Several of the *Left Behind* characters were married, which again is a use of creative license that needs to be carefully guarded by the authors. The 144,000 will evangelize the world in a relatively short time, as Matthew 24 and Revelation 7 also indicate. The compact nature of their conversion to Christ, and the greatest evangelical movement in human history will be startling to say the least. Will the 144,000 have only a little knowledge of Eschatology? Probable. Will they have little knowledge of Christ? Possible. That doesn't mean that the basics of our Belief won't be active in their messages. Their message might be stark and brief, something I will discuss later. One needs to know that Christ is the answer for your sin and your salvation, placing all of your earthly trust upon Him. That will be enough.

God, from the foundation of the earth, foreknew the 144,000 and chose them (the Greek word is *Eklektos* – or elected). The Lord elected them for such a time as it will be. See how long-suffering and patient our Heavenly Father is? He waits for all to come to a saving knowledge of Him at their own correct time. When I first perceived this Biblical group in my studies, I began to see why God wants this future time to be seven years long.

You see, if He has already seen all that there is above or under the earth that ever will be, Jesus doesn't need more than a millisecond to judge the inhabitants of earth of their today sin or those of tomorrow. Frankly, I have already shown that He already judged the world of their sin before the foundation of the earth. But the reason why He allows mortals to walk through this future era of unbridled craziness is not just for wrath but to push people over the edge of truth. He wants your attention today, but Jesus will get it no matter what in the Tribulation if He has to! I am sure that all of you reading this book know of loved ones who are so close to the truth that you can taste their salvation, but they don't want a Faith to disrupt their lives as they are now.

This upturn of the world in the beginning of the Tribulation, a literal cleaning of the planet as one would a spring housecleaning, is just what Dr. Jesus ordered. There will be nothing to trust in during that time (banks, jobs, money or families). They will have so little knowledge (after the First Rapture) and be deserving of a few blows (meaning some level of tribulation because of their waiting – not because of their sin which was already paid for on the Cross). This is exactly the word used in Luke 12:48 "But the one who did not know and did things deserving of blows will be beaten lightly..." Those few blows will be a result of their lack of decision to follow Christ when they knew they should have before the first Rapture. They will suddenly *get it* and become ardent followers of the One, True God, led by the triumphant teaching of the best evangelism timeframe the world has ever seen with the 144,000 Jews (who also will fathom the mercy of God and His gift of Grace after the First Rapture).

Some will comment: "Hey, I thought the Jews were the Chosen of God in the Old Testament? Aren't you just using a fancy replacement theology?" Absolutely not! The Jews are blinded for a time (of which we will discuss later on as the Remnant). But as I mentioned earlier, we are all grafted onto the Vine in John 15. Consider this: does it really matter to the Lord that someone is conjoined to the Branch of Christ a little later than earlier? Is there a sin in there I am missing? Christ sees all of us already finished in Him no matter when he or she comes to Him.

Step into a Confusing Time

Let me create a fictional account to give you the understanding of what might be taking place for those who are left behind from the first Rapture. A wife, before the Rapture of the Faithful, falls in love with Jesus. She becomes sold out to Christ. The husband is semi-retired but cannot work due to his disability and is bitter about the injuries he has sustained during his blue-collar career. He takes care of the finances while at home. He accompanies his wife to Church at first for a few services but doesn't join in on the Bible studies where she finds her faith unveiled. She invites him many times, but he is more interested in NFL and MLB in their seasons. She allows him to indulge his sport's passions but knows that his heart is being dragged farther away from a saving knowledge each day he delays.

One morning, she is gone. He cannot find her and wonders why she might leave for work so early at four AM. As he calls her cell phone, he finds it is beside her bed by her Bible. For the next several days, he hears the newscasts of millions of people disappearing. He cannot believe that his wife has just left him alone, because she loved him. He considers the disappearances for different reasons and hopes that she hasn't fallen for another man.

As he continues to see the news footage that the people of the earth have departed in front of the camera's view, he becomes convinced by her continued absence, and the mounting evidence that she is truly gone from this earth. He finally accepts her fate as having left to be in Heaven. He wanders the city not sure what he is searching for, but vainly hopes that she may show herself with others who have hidden out at their Churches. The husband wonders if this Rapture idea might have some level of truth within it, as it has surfaced on the internet. His wife talked about that concept a time or two, but he didn't pay much attention to her. After peering at a flyer in a coffee shop which is sorely short-staffed, he decides to attend a meeting promising to uncover the truth of this Rapture theory. He thinks that it is better than staying at home in an empty house.

After hearing the evidence of a young man at the microphone who is passionate but raw in his presentation, the husband's heart is caught in the truth that the Rapture has occurred. The husband is convinced that his wife has gone to be with her Lord. Not knowing that he could have joined her in the Rapture of the Faithful, he makes the commitment to Christ as well.

Within months, his government looks nothing like what they once were, and the disability checks (not to mention his social security he depended so much upon) start to disappear from his direct deposit. The phone numbers he calls, as well as the websites he tries to surf, indicate that those who cannot contribute will not be fed (in the way that the government had the ability to do in the past). The entitlement payments are too great a price for an already taxed system to bear. What does he do with the time he has left upon the earth?

While this is fictional, it is not only possible but probable that this scenario plays itself out with similar detail. Luke 12:48 is a vivid picture of this husband's spiritual condition before his wife is Raptured. He knows little about Jesus, and what the final destiny of the Church is. His lack of faith was relatively apparent before the Rapture of the Church. It is painfully obvious to those who are left to fend for themselves that they will be caught flat-footed in the economic chaos.

That time in the beginning of the Tribulation will also have the worst inflation known to man which is encompassed in the Third Seal in Revelation 6:6. The basic foodstuffs of the world cannot be obtained without a massive amount of cash. But interestingly the luxuries for the super wealthy are still available as stated in the Third Seal. The Chosen and the 144,000 Tribulation Saints will "not live by bread alone but every word that proceeds from the mouth of God (Matthew 4:4)." There is hope for those who survive this time that they can be a part of the Rapture of Revelation 7:9 (other references to this are Rev.14:1, and Luke 12:38).

One of the most fascinating verses that has always been missing from Tribulation discussions applies to the Mid-Trib Rapture is 2 Peter 2:9: "Then the Lord knows how to rescue the godly from trials and to keep the unrighteous under punishment until the day of judgment..." Others use this verse as proof of a Post-Trib or Pre-Wrath Rapture, but I believe that it is more likely that the verse is talking to the Chosen and 144,000 since they will not see the severe trials, or that they will be Raptured in the Middle of the Tribulation. The next group of Believers will have to suffer as the world crisis spirals out of control: they can be referred to as the Called.

Chapter 15

THE CALLED, TWO WITNESSES, AND AN ANGEL OF THE LORD

Friend – These are the writers of the New Testament and Old Testament including prophets and disciples.

Faithful/Bride – This group leaves in the Pre-Tribulation Rapture.

Chosen and the 144,000 – 144,000 are the Jews saved in the beginning of the Tribulation who preach to the Chosen. Both are Raptured Mid-Tribulation.

Once you surmount the mental hurdle referred to as the Chosen group with some understanding of the patience of the Lord regarding humanity's lack of appreciation of what our Savior accomplished on the

Cross. We then must move forward to the next group is even more trying to our God's patience. After a second disappearance in Revelation 7:9 of the 144,000 and the Chosen (the Mid-Trib Rapture), the world will be missing more of its population than ever without a death to explain their passing. The conditions of the people of the world will change even more dramatically.

The Divisions of Humans and the Anti-Christ

There will be a man who will take up the mantle of the long feared figure of the Anti-Christ. He will be a real person before the Tribulation who has a Body, Soul and Spirit, since I believe that he is alive in our generation being somewhat close to his entrance into the world of politics. I am not putting a date on it because that makes no Biblical sense. But what I feel that there is an immanency of his arrival from the First Seal that Jesus will open up in the future. The Body of a person is self-explanatory in its physical nature that is well known, but the Soul is slightly different when it encompasses one's Mind, Will and Emotions. The Mind houses the cognitive thought processes that make us the way that we are and how we access our brain functions. The Will is the reason why we get out of bed when we don't really want to; the reason that we start and keep a business going when the tough times come (trust me, it's hard). Our Will aids us to continue to choose to love someone who isn't loveable at the time (an adult child who has gone astray in life, for instance). You might believe the last one is an emotion, but anyone who has had to love a spouse or child who is difficult to interact with knows that love is not an emotion, but it is a choice which has more to do with your Will than anything else.

Your Emotions sometimes dictate how you react or

do not react in a critical situation. When you place all those raging Thoughts, Emotions and Will together, we have the personality or the individuality of the Soul. The Spirit is exemplified so well by Bob Yandian with his teachings upon this topic. Pastor/Teacher Yandian gives his listeners the understanding that the Spirit is alive at birth as noted by Proverbs 20:27. I used to believe, as he mentions back in the eighties in his own investigation of the Spirit, that the Spirit was dead in a young human, then becomes alive in a life once we have been reborn as in John 3 when Jesus is talking about Nicodemus. Pastor Bob explains that the Spirit is more like a candle in the young child who is burning down until it feels the death inside (or the wick running out). It has to be replaced by the gift of God with a lamp that has oil within it (well discussed in Matthew 25 in the amazing parable about the 10 Virgins). The Spirit would be alive in the born-again Christian, and once that rebirth occurs, it is seated in Heavenly places.

What does all of this have to do with the Anti-Christ? Jesus, after the Church leaves the earth when Jesus takes His Bride home, allows the Anti-Christ to be introduced to the world (2 Thess. 2:7-8 and in the opening of the First Seal in Revelation 5). Those left do not know what hits them, and then this charismatic man comes on the scene to solve the ills of the people by creating peace in the Middle East with Israel who will be on the war path after being attacked, as prophesized, in the Ezekiel 38-39 War. The Anti-Christ, no longer deterred by the Church on the earth, then can swoop in to create a seven-year peace with Israel (Daniel 9:27). Revelation 13:11-14 talks of the first beast (the Anti-Christ) that comes from among the people in obscurity, as does the False Prophet later explained in the same chapter. There are some who think they have identified the Anti-Christ or the False Prophet today but Scripture tells us through 2

Thessalonians 2:7-8 that the man of Lawlessness cannot be revealed until we are taken out of the way.

The Anti-Christ then has the Spirit and the Soul of the Beast inside of him as well, also explained in Revelation 13. The Beast, a demon, has periodically entered the world to take over world leaders throughout history (first explained by the prophet Daniel), possibly Satan's way to control the direction of humanity which has come into the world at least four times before. Each time this Beast introduces himself to the world scene, he kills and destroys whole populations (study the four beasts from Nebuchadnezzar to Alexander the Great and so on). This is one bad Spirit. He indwells the Anti-Christ to start the Tribulation. Some believe that the Anti-Christ is only indwelled after he is wounded, but I would say that Bible evidence supports that the Beast indwells him before Satan does and through Devil's command. This Satanic access makes the world worse than anything we can imagine in the first 3.5 years of a time of ugliness.

In the middle of this timeframe of seven years, Daniel indicates that the Anti-Christ will be wounded, Revelation 13:14, fatally. Some believe that he will be killed and then is raised from the dead, while others feel that he might not be literally killed, but either consequence is not clearly indicated, nor does either consequence matter enough to argue. Satan then enters the Anti-Christ's Body in a crowded consciousness in which the Beast still occupies, meaning that as many as seven separate parts of the nature of entities are inside of the Anti-Christ (Anti-Christ's Body, Soul, and Spirit; Beast's Soul and Spirit; and finally, Satan's Soul and Spirit).

When the Satan-filled Anti-Christ strolls into the Temple to accomplish the Abomination that causes Desolation, it will again be uglier than the world can realize. Abomination, in Greek, intimates the sickest of idol worship that denigrates a life-giving place (the Temple of God) into a desolate place spiritually. Then the gloves come off upon humanity. First off, he is going to require the Mark of the Beast to buy and sell and will allow the False Prophet to kill anyone who is unwilling to worship the First Beast. Instead of your credit cards or even cash, this number will be placed on your right hand or forehead for the chip readers to scan your financial and health information.

This Mark is a once and for all decision. If anyone takes this Mark, it is like a death penalty but only for your Soul; it's impossible to undo your life once you die. That's why the Word clearly identifies how important the Body's life is in making a choice for or against Christ during one's life. There are many people who are fearful that they will unknowingly take the Mark of the Beast. Trust me, you will know when that occurs. But again, the Bride, the Chosen and the 144,000 are not here!

The Two Witnesses

The Two Witnesses are somewhat confusing for Prophecy teachers, relating to who they are and when they come back to the planet. Some put these ancient characters in the first half of the Tribulation. I personally believe that their message gives us a clue as to their timeframe. These Two, alive for only three and a half years, consistently preach about a judgment, which means that they therefore cannot be around for more than half of the seven-year period. It is my belief that they exist in the second half of the Tribulation based upon their message. A fascinating addition is that both the 144,000 and the Two Witnesses are sealed of Christ and cannot be killed. We explained the immense significance to this finding releasing the 144,000 to be Raptured off of the earth. But the Two Witnesses are also given that same marking of God, so that they cannot be harmed.

The people on the earth will have some level of distress in the first portion of the Tribulation as we discussed in the last chapter. The second half is deadly as it conforms to the analogy of the world circling the proverbial drain. I have heard many Prophecy teachers identify the Two Witnesses as Moses and Elijah, but since Moses died a physical death, I find that unlikely. The reason for this conclusion is Hebrews 9:27: "And just as it is appointed for people to die once, and after this judgment." Paul, the purported writer of the book of Hebrews, gave the indication that people cannot live more than once. This philosophically disproves those who adhere to a reincarnation viewpoint, therefore, I believe that this puts to bed Moses as one of the Two Witnesses.

We have already indicated the potentials of the Two Witnesses as Enoch and Elijah who are the best two that I think fit the bill to preach to this final group of Souls coming to a saving knowledge of Jesus as the Called. I feel that the Called will not actually respond to truth as the other groups (the Faithful and Chosen) who hear about God. They need a stronger message. The Two Witnesses, as Enoch and Elijah speak in their own prose, are characterized as two men who pierce into the heart of those who listen to their message like very few before or after, other than the power of Isaiah.

Sin and Slaves

Luke 12:47 indicates a chilling message: "And that slave who knew his master's will and didn't prepare himself or do it will be severely beaten." A slave (*doulos*) is such an interesting word to use here but is similar throughout the verses of Luke 12:41-48 speaking of stewards and servants. We are all slaves to Christ. Exodus 21:2-6 indicates that a man who is taken into slavery has few choices. He must serve the master for six years, in the Hebrew tradition. After his term is served, if he arrives alone, he leaves alone. But if the master gives him a wife and he states that he loves his master, wife and kids, then the slave has a choice to be a *doulos* for life. The judge over that city takes the *doulos* to a doorpost, and his master pierces his ear with an awl. That slave is then marked with that earring as a sign to all that he has chosen to remain in the master's household. As an Audiologist studying these verses, I believe that it is not placed in the fleshiest portion of the ear as modern choices indicates as the earlobe. I believe that the awl is pierced into the painful portion of the concha bowl that is in the cartilage section for more permanence.

We also have the strange statement in Revelation which talks about an Angel of the Lord flitting about the planet pushing the Gospel message. Some Prophecy teachers, including me for a very long time, had difficulty believing that it was one personality that would seek the Called inside of billions of potentials, but I have dropped that idea. Here is the concept of one's feeling about the Word as opposed to what it says about itself. If the Scriptures indicate one angel, I think I will go with the Lord and His foresight. I have no concept of how that will play out, but I cannot wait to see how that one angel will evangelize from the physical realm so brazenly. It's one of the very few examples within the Bible of an angel being visible throughout the planet.

Most times, an envoy from the Lord comes to proclaim his point and move away after he is done. I believe that it is highly possible that he will be visible again and again as the powers of this world become more evil and murder spreads at wildfire rates. That angel will the forces of our God to gather the lost.

When one studies my favorite above chapter of Luke 12, without a full understanding of the groups, these verses are relatively difficult to comprehend. The reason for Prophecy teachers' confusion resides inside of judgment. Again, if you perceive the End Times as a judgment upon sin, then these verses talk about different people within the Bride. Some are not ready for Christ and need to be beat up for their sin. What this implies is the notion that we must suffer for our sins, so that we may be made perfect inside of our persecution to eradicate the sin from our lives. Therefore, if we are able to purge our Flesh of sin by ourselves, what real need do we have for the blood of Christ?

Mormons give their adherents an answer to this proposition in that a person is given grace over one's sin if he accepts the Mormon Jesus at his first time to confess. But he must spend his life trying to work out his salvation by killing off sin or giving confession/recompense to those sins. If you are already dizzy by these big nasty words, you are not alone. Even Martin Luther was there for a long time until he realized that sin's payment was accomplished in the finished work of the Cross.

The truth of the Gospels and Paul's writing makes it clear that we cannot do anything to attain the blood redemption of Christ short of us confessing sin. But what about when we sin as a Believer? When we confess the sin that we have committed today, it's not to make us sinless again. I know that is almost heresy in most churches who believe the opposite. Our sin puts us in poor standing without our relationship with Jesus. All we are doing is righting our relationship.

If I tick Wendy off by being a jerk in our marriage, does she cease to love me and want a divorce right away? Some actually exist in this type of fear in their marriages. That's not how Christ operates with us. He is faithful to forgive us of all of our unrighteousness once we start the ball rolling in confession (admission of our poor ways against Him in I John 1:9).

Therefore, my comment about these groups of people in Luke 12 is that all of them are inside of the Body of Christ. They just learn of their Faith at a different time in their journey. One who can accept Christ when there is no evidence of His return to the earth (the Bride) receives a bridal shower and wedding to the Lamb. Those who take their sweet time to pony up to the confessional bar only after there is more evidence that the Bible is coming true in front of their eyes will find that their lack of decision-making at the easier time costs them in "blows." The more the blows, the later the timeframe which is why we see the Chosen taking only a few blows because they come to Christ after the first Rapture (of the Bride) and not later. When we come to the Called, we watch a more stubborn response to the prompting of Christ.

Back to the Called

1 and 2 Thessalonians spend a huge amount of time dealing with the End Times. It must be noted that these books were written near the beginning of Paul's mission after his conversion and training. In I Thessalonians 1:6, it states that "You became imitators of us and of the Lord when, in spite of severe persecution, you welcomed the message with joy from the Holy Spirit." This is indirectly speaking of the Thessalonians in what they were experiencing, but Paul referenced these several other times making a parallel between it and a group of severely persecuted *Hagios* (Saints). Remember, Scripture has layers of

evidences within it to give a timeless reader an ability to identify themselves within the passage, as well as the one whom it will finally come to which I believe the above refers to the Called.

Anyone who will live in the last half of the Tribulation will see significant persecution up to and including death. At that future time, the Mark of the Beast will be required for all citizens of the world, as well as the allegiance sworn to the Beast who houses the Satanic Anti-Christ. Through him, Satan will make war against the Saints, and the people of God which are the Jews living at the time. Scripture, in several places, indicates that Israel, by the end of the Tribulation, will have less than a third of their own population worldwide alive due to this severe persecution.

Severely Beaten and Destined for a Purpose

The words *severely beaten* in Luke 12:47 indicates martyrdom, in that the wording means *poly* or many, *thrashing* or flaying. And of course, the Called will be a people who are on the slate to be killed, because they have a destiny in this timeframe due to their opposition against the ruler of the world. They will oppose the Anti-Christ more, not in their ability to make war against him in a physical way, but by living in opposition of him upon the earth. Satan comes down from Heaven with "great wrath" trying to take out anyone who doesn't want to bow to him (Rev. 12:12). This Revelation verse gives us the understanding that Satan is after everyone, because he knows his time is short. He will never rule the world in the way that he used to under Ephesians 6 where he is and was the ruler of the air. A trapped adversary is one of the most dangerous opponents that one may have. That is where Satan will find himself.

My study of the Called was one of the most fascinating ever encountered other than a disturbing group referred to as the Goats. The Called is referred to obliquely in Romans 8:28-30. These verses refer to the Called three separate times and follow the word Called with *purpose*. Of course, all Christians are *called* according to His purpose. The Lord has a plan for all His creation when we choose for Him. This can simply, on the surface, be applied to the all believers in Christ of all times. But I believe that it has a dualistic meaning, as we have discussed earlier that there are many deeper semantics in Scripture. Listen to the nature of these very descriptive verses:

> *We know that all things work together for the good of those who love God: those who are called according to His purpose. For those He foreknew, He also predestined to be conformed to the image of His son, so that He would be the firstborn among many brothers. And those He predestined, He also called; and those He called, he also justified; and those He justified, He also glorified.*

These amazing verses have so much to tell us that we could not complete their meaning in a two-hundred-page document. But it is interesting that the world has argued over Predestination and Free Will, as described earlier, for hundreds of years. Could it be possible that God, in His foreknowledge as He lays out above concepts, has given a much more defined path for the Called in the time called Jacob's Trouble (Jeremiah 30:7)? I do not believe that God limits any person's Will. But the consequence of the person's lack of choice for Christ subjects the person to all manner of death that culminate the potential for all flesh to die (Matt. 24:22) if the End Times were extended by just a few more days. It is just like our Lord to give a special protection since there will be an open season upon those who choose Christ against the Anti-Christ. Called, in Greek, is translated from *Kaleo* which means to bid forth. I guess as I consider this group in the same vein as in the times I was called to the principal's office. A teacher might kick me out of her classroom (it didn't happen too many times due to my terror of the event) and send me to the chairs outside of the principal's office at Pine Lane Elementary in Parker, Colorado. I would sit awaiting my fate of which I could imagine humiliations and screaming galore. Making that little Scott wait outside of the Principal's office was the best part of the potential punishment as it is for any child. As the child lingers upon the throne of despair, most serve up their guilt for our actions so easily for a nice Principal to counter any further punishment other than a direct scolding. In taking this blighthing analogy, I am not trying to under value blood that will be spilled by the Called in those last three-and-a-half years before the Kingdom commences. But consider that these people will have had plenty of time to see the truth without choosing the obvious.

Called – Didn't Prepare Themselves

The name Called gives the understanding of something set-aside for purpose, as the shew bread in the Temple is sliced by the priests. Putting these two Greek words (Called and Purpose) together indicates that God has a reason for bringing them together for such a time as this. But if we work deeper in Luke 12:47, we see that this group knew the master's will but didn't prepare himself or do it, and "will be severely beaten." Two portions of this verse that indicate this group the best are the words *prepare* and *know* their master's will. The word for prepare is *Hetoimazo* which also means to make ready for necessary preparations.

As an Audiologist in Tulsa, we have many people who congregate at the gun shows. I have been around guns all my life and had believed that I understood the position of gun owners until I frequented the guns shows professionally (we sold custom ear protection to those gun owners). There were so many wearing camouflage at these gun shows that I wondered where the foliage with which to blend was placed. Ex-Vietnam and ex-Iraqi war vets were only two of the types of males that attend these shows. They spend thousands of dollars in cash for ammo and heavy weapons. It was not uncommon to see AK-47's slung upon the shoulders with a pipe sign sticking out of the barrel explaining the type of weapon and the requested amount in cash. There were so many variations of prepping gear imaginable in a large auditorium from water systems to dehydrated food, besides all the weapons.

The Prepping personality was critical for me to study in *Foretold Book Two* series in which I was documenting the characteristics of this eclectic group. There are whole compounds which people pay hundreds of thousands for a fully stocked underground shelter with maybe only a few hundred square feet to hide them from the wrath of humanity. What I also didn't know is that it is considered good preparation for individuals to have as much as a two-year of supply of water, power, food and ammo for a coming Armageddon. The problem that most people haven't understood in America is that Armageddon doesn't mean what they think it means. Most believe that it is a final battle in which humanity dukes it out and only a few live to tell their tales. Most Pre-Wrath prophecy teachers are selling their wares upon the broadcasts or internet. Water purification to dehydrated supplies are favorites among this group. Do they know and believe in the End Times as Luke 12:47 indicates? Yes, they do. The Chosen do not believe in the end of the world (neither necessarily the destruction as the movies portray or a final seven-year countdown). The Called absolutely do believe in a final countdown and prepare for it. The problem with this position is they believe that one can be *Off the Grid*, so that the government cannot come after you and your supplies are sufficient to survive.

Firstly, no one is really *Off the Grid*. If you drive a newer car less than twenty-years old, have a social security number, pay taxes, use a cell phone, communicate by email, or any other form of commerce, you are in the government's system. They can find you. The sites that might be considered out of the way of business routes are already understood to be frequented by those who might oppose federal controls that will surely change in the last seven years of the world's history.

Next, this group misses a key point to Bible prophecy. Any one of the Trumpet or Bowl wraths, not to mention a potential Seal judgment, could wipe out all the years of preparation. They include the burning of all the green grass, a comet that makes the seas bitter, and more trashing of the fresh water sources and hailstones that fall as blood. If anyone has a fresh water aquafer, their location could be toast in a Biblical moment. Within a week, the Prepper would have to pack up and leave without fresh water available to his family. All the years of preparation would be for naught.

God is seeking to disrupt human dependency upon itself. The Tribulation's primary purpose is to make each person on the earth choose for Christ or against Him. There is no middle ground; no atheistic views and none in foxholes (this phrase, usually attributed to American journalist Ernie Pyle in 1942, was also attributed to Douglas MacArthur or William Cummings). There will be no person upon the face of the planet who will *not* know that God is directing the paths of His whole creation (Romans 1:19). They will feel the wrath of the Lamb.

But I also believe that He is showing patience upon humanity as well. 2 Peter 3:9 says, "The Lord does not delay His promise, as some understand delay, but is patient with you, not wanting any to perish but all to come to repentance." This is one verse that most do not read correctly. The next verse exclaims about the *Day of the Lord* will come like a thief. That is clearly discussing the End Times and not just about today (of course I would hope that those reading this book understand that "today is the day for salvation"). Jesus could choose to get it over with fast, but He is seeking all who may come to Him. He has already foreknown who would come to a saving knowledge of Him.

The Called's Rapture

Even though those Believers are in the Called category during those last years, there is hope that He is long-suffering and is waiting for the hardening of their hearts. Revelation 14:16 is one of the most misinterpreted verses by Pre-Trib Prophecy teachers, because they do not perceive the totality of the verses around it. "So, the One seated on the cloud swung His sickle over the earth and the earth was harvested." This is a direct quote of how Jesus will bring the Called into the Kingdom, but by a more violent means that any other harvest (we will explore the three harvests and how they relate to the three Raptures later). Verse 17 states "Then another angel who also had a sharp sickle came out of the sanctuary in heaven."

Most teachers place verse 16 with the rest, but there are critical differences to consider. Jesus is crowned King of the earth and in Heaven which is different than when He comes for His Bride in the first Rapture. Now, of course we already know that Jesus is the King of all. But verse 16 indicates that Jesus is in the clouds the crown adorned upon His head. Why? Because He is now married to His Bride. Many ancient traditions require that a prince (ours is the Prince of Peace) procure a wife before he takes the throne. His throne He is coming for is upon the earth and He is sitting in the clouds to take another portion of the Believers away with Him.

In verse sixteen, Jesus' coming occurs in the clouds to gather the last people to be Raptured. The other angels, in the later verses, come to trample the grapes. Grapes have two basic uses: life-giving as a fruit and wine to get drunk (Proverbs 20:1 state that "wine is a mocker; beer is a brawler"). The uses for wine, in the Old Testament, are argued by some scholars as helpful to the digestive system, but do not miss the point that wine of past ages was much less fermented and was needed due to the lack of pure drinking water. Jesus is taking His righteous grapes to Heaven, while the angels are judging (sent by God from the throne room) to bring about the righteousness that needs to cover the earth at the last part of the Tribulation (approximately in the last ten days). I believe that this is a picture of Rosh Hashanah.

Rosh Hashanah and the Called

In the original teachings of the Jews, Rosh

Hashanah, along with its counterpart holiday of Yom Kippur, are the most-high holy days in the Jewish calendar. Rosh Hashanah will be the day of acceptance of the Messiah as the Jewish King. That means that all Jews are waiting for prophecy to be fulfilled by the Messiah upon the first High Holy Day. In ancient times, enemies of Israel would come out and blow the Shofar to call them to worship God and then slaughter the Jews. Therefore, they instituted a policy that only the priests of God could initiate this celebration of the King, so that it was not exactly predicted to the day of the people. It is related to the new moon and the timing that occurs in the middle to late September, so it is fascinatingly called "The day that no man knows." Some erroneously, with the above information, believe that the Rapture of the Church (Faithful) occurs on this day; I used to believe this way as well due to the spiritual significant of Rosh Hashanah and its sister high holy day of Yom Kippur.

Rosh Hashanah will occur at the Tribulation period, not the beginning of it. The Shofar will be blown 100 times which is a Jewish indication of a Complete Blessing. That means that the *Blessing* of God, also indicated in Revelation 1:3 discussed above, is the three Raptures of believers which conclude with Rosh Hashanah with the Righteous going up in the Grape Harvest.

The Jews believe that there are three groups of people that exist at the time of what I am indicating as the Grape Harvest or Rosh Hashanah: the righteous, the wicked and the intermediate. Those three groups must interact with their destinies inside Jewish tradition. Revelation 22:11 intimates a chilling comment "Let the unrighteous go on in unrighteousness; let the filthy go on being made filthy; let the righteous go on in righteousness..." This is a reference that is fulfilled at the end of the Tribulation and an indirect indication of Rosh Hashanah

Celebrations.

The Unrighteous go into their death which is the winepress of God's wrath (Revelation 14:17 talk of those angels accomplishing the winepress); the Righteous would then be the Called that come into the Heaven during the final Rapture before wrath, or Pre-Wrath Rapture. The Unrighteous would be those who made their decision against Christ, most likely that they have chosen the Mark of the Beast sealing their fate. The Righteous would be the Called we have been discussing in this chapter. Again, no one is righteous due to their behavior (when considering their hard-heartedness), but they are only because of what they believe in Jesus. The Called come to a saving knowledge of the one true God. It all fits together because all Scripture is God-breathed, approved for teaching (2 Tim. 3:16).

Lastly, I must explain that most of the Called group will probably not make it to the final Rapture. Why? The Anti-Christ will be aiming for them without relenting. Most, I believe, will be martyrs. They will be the greatest group of martyrs for Christ the world has ever seen. We will be applauding their bravery in Heaven. Their testimony for Christ will bring all Heaven to tears. I know I will be bawling my eyes out in joy watching their witness.

Chapter 16

THE SHEEP AND THE GOATS

Friend – These are the writers of the New Testament and Old Testament including prophets and disciples.

Faithful/Bride – This group leaves in the Pre-Tribulation Rapture.

Chosen and the 144,000 – 144,000 are the Jews saved in the beginning of the Tribulation who preach to the Chosen. Both are Raptured Mid-Tribulation.

Called – the second to last group of people to be saved in the second half of the Tribulation. They are Preppers.

Some people will now be exclaiming that they have never heard of the above written groups before; they cannot imagine them as real separations that the Lord knows. But let me give you a hint what huge conflicts actually do to the world. World war change the attitudes of the world during the fight. Technology, fields of study (Audiology began after WWII), and huge concepts were introduced as well as the idea of the generations. That is similar to how these groups will form during the Tribulation as well as their identities.

The Rapture of the Bride along with even bigger global wars with nuclear tipped missiles with gigantic destructive forces will segment the nations into unique factions as well as changing how one sees his or her own life. Is it really that difficult to understand how the Called, Chosen and Faithful within the Believers that will inhabit each moment on this earth will arise? Can you now imagine that the world will hunt down Christians to torture them just because they do not worship the Anti-Christ? If you are considering the groups I have described then you have an inkling of how much our world would adjust with the new forces riding rough shod over their perceptions.

The Goat Response

I would be remiss if we left out the two most difficult groups to quantify: The Sheep and Goats. I attended a Christian business conference in Colorado Springs with Andrew Wommack's ministry under Charis Bible College. Dr. Lance Wallnau made several references to the Sheep and Goat nations in his talks relating to the nations that exist today. While his references aren't exactly what I believe God is trumpeting in the End Times, he did make several good points (Dr. Wallnau wasn't wrong. He was extending a Biblical concept and borrowing it for his analogies, which was completely fine for consistent parable-type teaching).

Today, the only two groups that exist are the Faithful and the unbelieving Goats. We already discussed who the Faithful are, but we must explain more about the Goats being the group which do not believe in the Gospel. The Called are preppers and until the Tribulation period, this group doesn't believe in the Jesus of the Bible. This does not mean that all preppers don't believe in the Jesus of the Bible, but the Called are a future group of people who, at this point, are not counted among the Bride because of their choice not to believe. Some of these future Preppers will accept Him during the second half of the Tribulation as we discussed in the last chapter. The Chosen or the 144,000 also don't exist as a group today, because we would attribute them possibly to surface Christians or unbelieving Jews respectively. But the Church is here working on this earth who have not seen Christ but believe in Him as their Groom. The Goats, on the other hand, have already taken off their perceived yokes that bind them, because Fundamental Christianity just doesn't meet their needs.

We, as an American culture, don't like to believe in the Bible. Many claim that "it's filled with errors; it's metaphorical in nature." I have a friend named Mark. He and I used to lead a Bible Study together in high school along with our friend, Scott, whom I mentioned earlier. Mark now indicates through Facebook that he doesn't believe in the Word, and that it has been tampered with over the years. His comments are commanding but relatively aimless, because he has no basis for what he believes.

There are Preachers whose whole job is to explain a book written millennia before their time, consistently state that the message was given down through the Monks of the 1500's and earlier which has been misinterpreted. They believe that it cannot really be trusted and is unknowable as to its original intent. The Bible has not been changed and is older than these supposed scholars wish to admit, however.

But these rewriters of history need to be seen as only one thing: heretics. They unfortunately have a special place in hell, according to God's book.

In Luke 17:2, Jesus warns that if one child is led astray by poor teaching that "it would be better to be thrown into the sea with a millstone around your neck." No other group is given this much venom in Jesus' spoken Word, who spoke so candidly about the Pharisees and Sadducees. These teachers placed law upon law into the people's spiritual knapsack making their burden too heavy to carry. They misrepresented the Old Testament in adding to the common people's confusion as to their access to God. The Old Testament Priests were not intended to be a barrier to the Father, but tradition derivated their roles. Unfortunately, those same types of people exist today in the Goats.

Understanding my Goat Dream

I had a dream in 2015 that startled me to my core. I caution the reader that my wife in real life has *nothing* to do with the illustration that the dream was invoking. She has been with me faithfully for more than 25 years. In this dream, I will quote how I wrote it in November 14, 2015:

> *My wife had left me after the first year or so of being married. I hadn't been in contact with her for some time. I was distraught by her departure from my life. She then gave me a written notice to attend her party. She walked into an upper room with only the skimpiest of lingerie with the sleaziest of friends trailing her. She was getting married to a muscled-bound man who dwarfed me in an effort to shame me. She*

began to compare me to him in every way possible. There were also a few other men who were at the party who began to compare themselves to me overwhelming my perceptions of my own physique.

She decided that she had enough of verbally abusing me, so her wedding party retired to the basement to perform their disgusting marriage service; I was to be upstairs for the laughs of the crew.

After a sleepless night, her wedding party came to mock me more to my utter embarrassment. I then yelled for her to "vomit, vomit, vomit" until she turned on the stairs clearly hurling all she had within her. I went downstairs to the foundation to see nothing of value.

What did I learn about this dream that had any insight upon the Goats? Plenty. Firstly, I again stated that this dream had nothing to do with my wife in any way, because she would never act this way, nor does she have any mocking friends. God was juxtaposing me with how Christ feels when His people, or the Goats, reject Him. He was letting me sense His pain in the dream. When the Goats denounce Him, it is considered adultery and is seen in this same light as my dream. The words of this woman in the dream would easily be words that many of those who have left the Church speak when de-confessing what Christ does in the spiritual or physical realm from His first coming to the planet.

Revelation 16:15 epitomizes this dream the best for me: "Look, I am coming like a thief. The one who is alert and remains clothed, so that he may not go around naked and see his shame is blessed." Then we also have Luke 13:26-28 where some of the wedding guests, Goats, try to show up for the table at the Lord's wedding feast. Here is a powerful clothing analogy that is reminiscent of Revelation 19:6-8 with the Bride having a new robe of Righteousness. Goats would have had a place at the banquet but chose against it to defile their clothes or maybe even to take them off. Revelation 3:18 sums the Goat's clothing best "I advise you to buy from me gold...and white clothes so that you may be dressed and your shameful nakedness not be exposed..." These people believe in the adultery of other religions, or in some form of mocking Christianity (on top of them floating inside of the world's hubris and will bring about ruin by their own actions). God has tremendously harsh words for this group (Luke 8:18, Luke 6:49, Matt. 25:41, Matt. 25:12 and Luke 12:46). You will not want to be anywhere near them on the day that Jesus separates the Sheep from the Goats just after the Great Day of the Lord in-between the end of the Tribulation and the beginning of the Millennial Reign of Christ (Matt. 25:32-33).

The Goats are just like the Church of Laodicea in Revelation 3:15-16: "I know your works, that you are neither cold nor hot. I wish that you were cold or hot. So, because you are lukewarm, and neither hot nor cold, I am going to vomit you out of my mouth." They choose the middle path not wanting to antagonize anyone but offending the only One who really matters. They never fully choose for Christ.

The Goats are an unseemly group, because most of Christianity believes that they can or cannot lose their faith depending upon their view of eternal salvation. While this isn't the place within this book to fully explore the Goats and their spiritual state that it needs, let's delve into a few options.

How do we know that Goats may be Believers at one time? They have a new Spirit. In the analogies of Matthew 25 of the parable of the Talents with the man who buries his one Talent and is sent to Outer Darkness. They are also called the Foolish Virgins. These types of parables indicate that Jesus has given them their clothes of Righteousness cloaked inside of the metaphors of a new lamp and then a Talent in the other extension.

But why do they drain out their oil? Oil is the Holy Spirit and when our lamp doesn't burn anymore, we cannot use our lamp for its intended purpose. The Word is the semantic extension of the oil. These Goats don't have the Word in them anymore by their own choice. Their salvation hasn't been taken from them without their permission; it's given away by their own choice. That's going to throw the Predestinationalist for a loop, but the Word is speaking for Himself. Why did I use that extension? The Word is alive and active (Heb. 4:12). It needs to be inside of the Believer.

Sheep Finding their Shepherd

Let's now examine the Sheep. When I consider the Pre-Wrath Rapture doctrine as the only Rapture, one of their hardest roadblocks comes in the form of the who? Who will enter the Kingdom of the earth or the Millennial Reign of Christ? If Jesus is taking all the Christians (or as Revelation states the Tribulation Saints) from off the world, who are the Bride going to govern upon the earth when Christ asks for us to Rule and Reign with Him? Another way to say it is this: if God Raptures all of the Saints at that end point, it means that they change into non-physical beings in which do not have the ability to marry or have kids (Matt. 22:30). Some of the adherents state that it will be the Jewish Remnant. This is partly correct since the last third left upon the earth who are Jewish will cry out to God at Rosh Hashanah as we stated, but so will the Sheep.

In Zechariah 14:16, "Then all the survivors from the nations that come against Jerusalem will go up year after year to worship the King, the Lord of Hosts, and to celebrate the festival of Booths." This will occur during the Millennial Reign. This verse is packed with statements that need to be considered. We think of the word *survivors* as those who just happened to live through a tragedy. But *Yatar* also means that God has preserved them, or they remained upon the planet in bodily form. Don't you believe that the Lord of Hosts has a plan for all of His creation? He absolutely does! The Sheep will bow at the same time that the Jews will in those last ten days before He steps onto the planet in the aforementioned Rosh Hashanah when Jesus shows up in the clouds with a crown on to claim the earth. Too many do not focus on the word *Nations,* but instead the word *survivors.* They will not be Jews, because someone will have to come to Jerusalem to worship the Father each year at the Jewish feasts. The Feast of Booths (or Tabernacles) will be a unique ceremony in which the people will gather outside in tents and tell of the great things that the Lord has done for them. The Sheep will live through the whole Tribulation, including the last ten days of wrath. They never chose to accept Jesus, when they could have been Raptured with the Called in the Revelation 14:14, Grape Harvest, as we have discussed.

The Sheep will be a critically blind group. But you must hear some of the real-world stories of the animals (sheep and goats) to know more about the wonderful analogy that ties the group to the animals that they represent. A teacher named Dr. Lance Wallnau had an experience that he shared with a group of a few hundred people at Charis Business Meeting in Woodland Park, CO in 2016. He told of a story about a woman raising sheep and goats. The goats tend to meander upon the slight inclines overlooking their territory. Once they find something that they want, they nudge the sheep out of the way to pounce upon the food for themselves. I also have my own sheep and goat stories.

I raised two pigs per year over a three-year period from late grade school to early junior high. At the Douglas County Fair in Colorado every year, my pigs were set up in the goat and the sheep pens. We had a six by six area for our animals per person. I spent most of my time talking to my pigs and noticed that the goats would eat the pants off of you if you leaned up against their gates. They ingest anything around them whether it was edible or not.

Sheep, on the other hand, were slightly more picky but dumber than rocks. Sheep were completely unaware when the slaughter was coming. As the sale would complete the Fair for the year, the animals were herded away for slaughter. My pigs knew it; it was very emotional and a difficult task to coax them into the trucks to their doom. Goats were a little easier, I noted, but the sheep would go wherever you asked them to move as long as they were following their shepherd. The children who brought them to the Fair had spent months getting to know their little guys and could speak a word in a crowd to recognize the voice of their master (see Jesus' reference in John 10:2-9).

The Sheep of the Tribulation are the people who wander through the seven years, not understanding why they are doing what they are doing. They are blind for one reason or another, while everyone else seems to have a clue. They do not take the Mark and somehow survive to the end. Just like when I stated above about the Laodicean Church being spewed out of Jesus' mouth, the Sheep will sit dangerously close to the edge.

The Sheep are that Intermediate group that sees Jesus in the clouds at Rosh Hashanah before the last ten days of the earth as we know it in its corrupted form; I will explain that later in more detail about those two Holidays. They finally recognize His voice and bow down to Him in final reverence.

The Remnant Israel

The Remnant are very similar to the Sheep in almost every way, other than a few minor alterations to their destiny. Firstly, there have always been Jews upon this planet. They were without a homeland from 70 AD until their reformation in their physical boundaries in 1948. It is one of the cornerstones to prophecy, because Ezekiel 36-37 explain that the Jews would come back to life as a people and a nation in the last days. No ethic group has ever reconstituted themselves while having their language and most of their DNA intact.

After they are entreated in the beginning by the Anti-Christ for a seven-year period of supposed peace, he reneges upon his promises by moving into their temple. The Tribulation temple will be built sometime during the beginning portion of the Tribulation but has to be complete at least one year before the midpoint of the Tribulation. The Anti-Christ will set himself up in the temple as the god of this world, and that's when the really scary share of the seven years begins. As many as two thirds of the Jewish people will be hunted and killed during the last half of the Tribulation which leaves the final third of this group called the Remnant.

The Old Testament is replete with references of the Millennial Reign. The reason is that God promised Abraham an extended time of peace for His chosen people as the dominant race upon the planet in those one thousand years. It's not that the other nations, of whom I call Sheep, will not be around, as we have shared earlier, but they will be somewhat of a second tier to the primacy of the Jews. That's why Christians should keep the Jews in their own prayer life, because Jesus allowed for their ascendancy in His own supplications.

Therefore, the Remnant complete the same act seeing Christ in the clouds sealing themselves for 1000 years just one rung above the Sheep in the Millennial Kingdom. John 10:16 states that the Sheep hear His voice and become one flock. Jesus tells the world that He is laying His life down for all mankind. In 1 Corinthians 3:15, Paul teaches us that the man whose work is burned up will be lost, but "he will be saved; yet it will be like an escape through the fire." This is a scary indication like one who enters Heaven on his deathbed.

In a man's whole life, he could have followed his passions, but at his judgment of the Soul, his death, he receives the gift of grace that God gives him as he chooses God at that late point. All of his works, good, bad or indifferent are meaningless, because they are not done in Christ. He walks into Heaven with no knapsack or crown received other than a white garment of righteousness coming to the party late. I believe both the Sheep and the Remnant see the error of their ways at Rosh Hashanah when Jesus appears in the clouds to call all people to Himself (also the Called will be taken away in the third of the Raptures completing the trifecta of God's promises to those who come to know Him). John 19:37 has a verse that is from Zach. 12:10 "They will look at the One the pierced." While John was referring at first to the Cross of Christ, the Holy Spirit knew that Rosh Hashanah would be the oblique reference in which all view Jesus in the clouds.

The Sheep come to the party so late that Jesus cannot seat them at the Heavenly banquet table, but at least they get a seat upon the earthly banquet of the Millennium. They may die before that last ten days will be through, but if they survive, their reward will be green pastures where a lion may snuggle up to a lamb as a symbol of what they will be doing toward Jesus during the Millennial Reign of Christ. But this group answers the important question that is unresolved in the Post-Trib or Pre-Wrath position in the Great U-turn: who inherits the Kingdom? The Sheep and Remnant take up residence in the Millennial Reign. Do you see how God is always searching for another way to show His mercy?

Resurrected Believer's Job of Reigning

The Ruling and Reigning conversation over the Sheep is a difficult one to comprehend. One of the most generous women I have met is Jo Hovind of Creation Today Ministries. She has had many trials in her life but loves Jesus with all her heart. She struggled with the concept of the Believer's Ruling and Reigning with Christ. I told her of another way to consider our role in the Millennial Reign.

At the end of World War II, the Americans in March of 1945 came upon a site that they had only small glimpses in the weeks prior but nothing to the magnitude of Dachau. Six million Jews were killed during the Holocaust of WWII, but did you know that five million others were also killed? Gypsies, political prisoners, pastors, Russians, POW's and other enemies of the state. When General Dwight D. Eisenhower entered the camp of Dachau in Western Germany, he ordered the townsfolk to help the burial of the bodies.

The soldiers provided for the bedraggled creatures bereft of hope with more food they was possible. But the sudden caloric intake killed many of the starving Souls. The Physicians came in quickly to lock the prisoners back up into their camps to monitor their caloric intake slowly until their bodies could assimilate a correct diet for an adult. I truly believe that we are going to see something similar to this in our first few days back upon the earth in our resurrected bodies.

The Sheep and the Remnant of Israel will be in prison camps, tortured and at best, malnourished. I think it's at least possible for the next year that we will be handling the Post Traumatic Stress that all of humanity will have in their shaking bodies. They will need to be physically healed upon the planet to repopulate it again. Jo agreed that she would love to be a part of that regimen. God has a plan in place for all of us to participate.

Rapture: Could There Be More than One?

Chapter 17

THE WEDDING OF THE LAMB AND THE FEAST

Friend – These are the writers of the New Testament and Old Testament including prophets and disciples.

Faithful/Bride – This group leaves in the Pre-Tribulation Rapture.

Chosen and the 144,000 – 144,000 are the Jews saved in the beginning of the Tribulation who preach to the Chosen. Both are Raptured Mid-Tribulation.

Called – the second to last group of people to be saved in the second half of the Tribulation. They are Preppers.

Goats – Pastors and teachers who go astray and go

to Outer Darkness at the end of the Tribulation.

Sheep – Nations of Believers who accept Jesus after the last Rapture (Called) and live in the Millennial Reign.

Remnant – Final one third of Jewish survivors of the Tribulation who believe in Christ in the last ten days and live in the Millennial Reign.

I have given the sad groups of the Goats and the Sheep as well as revealed to you the Called (the Martyrs who will be among those who die in the faith, potentially a majority of the Called Believers in the Second Half of the Tribulation). Do you want some good news? Want something to look forward to? Here it is. The Wedding of the Lamb is so poorly understood by the Church that it bothered me for years. This is the real hope that we should be focusing upon. Wouldn't you like to know much more about your own future wedding? You can even know your Groom, too!

In Jewish tradition, a Friend introduces a single man to a virgin. That Friend knows exactly what his best friend wants in a Bride. He also knows the characteristics of the woman, so he is vouching for both sides. You guessed it - that Friend is the Gospel and Old Testament writers who introduce us to the Son, Jesus. But the Friend's job is not done yet.

Once the potential Groom meets the virgin, they have some time to get to know each other without sex. After the man decides that she is the one for him, he takes the moment to purpose in his heart that he will pay for her hand in marriage. He must pay a dowry of types to the father of the virgin. Here we have the *Pearl of Great Price* analogy in Matthew 13:45-46. Jesus spends all that He has to buy a field (all of humanity) for the pearl that is within it. In our case, the Bride accepts Him as her Groom.

The Father must then be compensated, because the woman is a part of His family (the business of the family to sustain itself). Then the Bride has the chance to accept the invitation to be His. That is our choice to have a new Spirit reborn in John 3. The dowry is paid to the Father, which is the death of Jesus. What else would a God give other than the only thing He wouldn't normally have? Death of His Son. The definition of God is eternal; therefore, He must give up His most precious gift of an eternal being: that is the life of our God.

Once she accepts to be His Bride, her job is to take that new lamp she is given (Spirit) in the transaction and put oil in it. She takes her burning lamp to her upper room to show the city that she is a virgin waiting for Him to come back for her. If the oil (the Holy Spirit in the Word) is not in the lamp, then she cannot show that she is Faithful. Don't you see? This is Matthew 25 played out for us! We read of the parable of the Foolish and Wise Virgins but didn't realize that this was a Wedding response for her waiting. There weren't cell phones to know when He was coming back. And He *IS* coming back.

He must build a house that is suitable for His Bride (John 14:3 in "I go to build a house for you..."). Inside of the Jewish tradition, the groom to be must build a house for his bride. It must be to the specs of the father and only thing may that groom retrieve his fiancé. That's the job of Jesus today as He builds our house in Heaven.

Now, if she has been faithful, she has shown that she kept the Holy Spirit in her lamp warding off the temptations of the world trusting that He was coming back (2 Peter 3:3). That's why we have the Foolish Virgins (Goats) who have a lamp but no oil (drained out the Word within their life and believed lies). Their place is in Outer Darkness (a shiver in your Spirit is practical here).

Once the Father tells the Son that His house is prepared for the woman of His dreams, the Son is released to go after His Bride. All over the Gospels, Jesus uses this analogy. But in Jewish tradition, the friends blow the trumpets when entering the town to indicate that the groom is coming into town (I Thess. 4:16-18 has the Pre-Trib Rapture within the trumpet blowing). That's a Wedding response, because she comes down from her perch to indicate her readiness for His coming. She kept the Word in her heart to feed her Spirit.

The traditional wedding is seven days long (read the beginning of Esther which backs up the seven day wedding and feast). That's why she has to come up seven years earlier than anyone else. She is called Faithful, because He was Faithful. The Bride is just taking on the last name that He has placed for her. Church, do you understand that when you call yourself Faithful in all things it's like when Wendy pulled her last name from Ellyson to Young to cleave to me? They have a private ceremony with the Father officiating (the Father creates the Will and the Law, but the Son executes the Father's Will) the Wedding between the two parties and the Friends witnessing it. That then is the consummation of the wedding.

Wedding Feast Explained

Here is one of the most confusing parts for any prophecy teacher, Matthew 22:1-14 (I recommend you open your Bibles to this passage and read along with what I write in the following sentences). On the surface, it seems relatively straightforward with the Father of the Groom talking to the guests and the servants (angels). But it is so much deeper than that.

I can see Jesus in my mind's eye Jesus gesticulating to express the depth of a story that only He has seen. Remember from the perspective of God, all things in Heaven have already occurred. The created beings just haven't experienced it yet. There are many characters within the drama of the event that will be the most glorious wedding in human history. Princess Diana's wedding will be nothing compared to this pageantry. Perry Stone expresses this wedding feast well. The Father walks among the guests of the feast which happens in the middle of the timeframe of feasting (Middle of the Tribulation). The Guests are the Chosen. They were Chosen from the Foundation of the Earth to see the Wedding of the Lamb in Heaven.

There are those who were Invited but didn't want to come. That's clearly the Called. Why? Verse 14 gives the clearest indication. "Many are Invited, but Few are Chosen." It's the same words we have used before here in the Wedding Feast analogy Jesus tells the world in Matthew. The Called are too stubborn to be a part of the Wedding Feast, and they miss it by going through the end of the Tribulation.

We also have the Goats who show up to the wedding without their wedding clothes on and naked, of which we have already shown. We also hear the Father passing judgment upon those who don't want any part of the Wedding in Heaven who are allowing their obstinance to destroy their lives. Those would be the people who took the Mark of the Beast who desire their own destruction with Satan. They understand the depth of their choice.

But we realize a bonus. Revelation 14 discusses the 144,000 Jews in Heaven having completed their task of bringing in the Guests or the Chosen. They have a song that no one can sing. I was the Wedding

Singer in many weddings and loved every second of it. I had a unique view of the proceedings. Don't you know that the Wedding needs the Singers? I can't prove this one, but it sure is interesting that Revelation 14 talks of the 144,000 having a song in Heaven that no one else can sing.

Chapter 18

THREE HARVESTS

Faithful/Bride – This group leaves in the Pre-Tribulation Rapture.

Chosen and the 144,000 – 144,000 are the Jews saved in the beginning of the Tribulation who preach to the Chosen. Both are Raptured Mid-Tribulation.

Called – the second to last group of people to be saved in the second half of the Tribulation. They are Preppers. The last Rapture is at Rosh Hashanah ten days before Jesus steps upon the earth. He is in the clouds.

Barley Harvest – Faithful Pre-Trib Rapture

There are three types of harvests we are going to explore, and the *whys* to each of the Raptures. While I am not going to try to impress you with my farming insight (of which my black thumb can attest), we can learn so much from the Bible's extended analogies of growing seasons, not to mention that it translates so effectively to every culture known to man throughout history. The first harvest is the Barley Harvest. When barley is harvested, the head of the stalk is removed to procure the barley grains. In ancient times, the process was not very physically demanding to extract the stem as it was then rubbed between one's hands to separate the chaff from the barley grains. This is similar to how God views the Faithful/Bride. There is a strong difference between the world and the Faithful, even though it might be difficult for us to perceive seeing all our faults.

But God states that the Unbelievers are *apistis*, which means un-faithful. We derive this same terminology from the word *atheist* which means that the person is a non-believer in a supreme God. So, the difference is stark in God's eyes. The *pistis*/Faithful, who are easily differentiated from the world, believe in Jesus in the way that Romans 10:9-10 states that the believer in Christ must accept Him as his or her Lord and Savior. Remember, Jesus recognizes you as a finished being, even though we have severe troubles viewing ourselves within that light. Again, if you are a Believer in the Word and Jesus, you *are* the Faithful Bride of Christ. Harvesting this group, in God's eyes, is more straightforward. Therefore, the Barley Harvest is representative of the Pre-Trib Rapture of the Bride right before the Tribulation.

Wheat Harvest – Chosen in Mid Trib Rapture

The Wheat Harvest is a little more labor intensive. In antiquity harvesting, the laborer took a simple device called a *Tribulum* after he cut the wheat stalk off the body of the plant, and then separated out the wheat grains on this threshing board. This *Tribulum* is the Greek for our word Tribulation. The wheat grains used for bread must be separated from the straw by rubbing against the *Tribulum*. Some people in this world cannot accept the Gospel in all its simplicity and dynamic range of wording without doubting whether or not it is historical. They see these Biblical stories and myths that are beautiful but not terribly relevant to their specific lives. Many seek proof or evidence before they will believe in the God of the universe coming down in the form of a human to die for sins that they struggle to notice are inside of us all.

The Chosen and the 144,000 need more evidence than the Church does to accept Christ. The 144,000 Jews will have a salvation experience potentially soon after the Faithful's Barley Harvest. Those Jewish converts will be able to show that the Bible predicted that the world would be turned upside down by a Pre-Trib Rapture. There are many people who don't believe that the Disciple John, or the other writers of the Bible, wrote what is inside of the modern pages we read today. Their incorrect perception is that the Word has been corrupted throughout the years with well-meaning people who could not transmit that information clearly and precisely.

My English professors worked voraciously to convince me of the futility of the Gospels in my undergraduate program. How could God have given this information to the world through the Bible correctly and those monks actually have repeated it accurately throughout the millennia? The Chosen will have tangible proof that the Bible has truth within it. That evidence will be all that they need to believe to become *Hagios* (Saints washed in the blood of Christ). But that doesn't preempt them from going through some tribulation as Luke 12:48 reflects. They will have some beating of their Bodies and Souls in this world gone mad, because they chose not to believe in Jesus before the Pre-Tribulation Rapture. Therefore, the second Harvest will be the Wheat with the Chosen Believers in Christ as the direct converts of the 144,000 Jewish young men around the middle of the Tribulation or a Mid-Trib Rapture.

Grape Harvest – Called in Pre-Wrath Rapture

The last group is the Grape Harvest of the Called. The Grape Harvest comes at Rosh Hashanah in the last ten days near the end of the Tribulation, just before many of final Bowls are poured out on those who have not accepted His grace to go in that final Rapture. Revelation 14:14-17 have an amazing account mixed in with two separate events that we mentioned in the last group of the wicked and the righteous.

The Grape Harvest is a much more violent process in that verse 14 "One seated on the cloud swung His sickle over the earth, and the earth was harvested." Where the Chosen needed a Tribulum to separate the wheat from the chaff, Jesus had taken His Bride to be with Him in the very beginning in the Barley Harvest. Jesus will come in the clouds to harvest the Called from the planet with His sickle. As Joshua had an elongated day in Joshua 10:11-13 in which the enemies of God were taken out by the Jews, so then will begin the last ten days upon the earth from Rosh Hashanah to Yom Kippur. Yom Kippur, or the Day of Atonement, seems to be eerily like the Great Day of Wrath which will be packed with so many occurrences that God will extend the day to deal with His enemies as well.

Of course, we never really deal with the Martyred in Christ here, do we? They are either the Chosen who have been persecuted to death or more likely the

Called who come to faith in Christ during that last half of the Tribulation. They are presented with the choice beyond all choices: die or accept the Mark of the Beast. The Martyred will have a straightforward option for them at that time – they choose death - even though you and I today cannot imagine the difficulty of the choice (although there have been Believers in this world who have experienced it up to the time of the Tribulation). I believe that they will be resurrected with the other Old Testament Saints in the beginning of the Millennium.

I promise you that in that hour of trouble, the choice for Christ or against Him will be clear. *The Left Behind* series by Jerry B. Jenkins and Tim LaHaye beautifully describe many of these type of martyr events in scary detail. Paul said it best in Philippians 1:21-23 "For me, living is Christ and dying is gain. Now if I live on in the flesh, this means fruitful work for me; and I don't know which one I should choose. I am pressured by both. I have the desire to depart and be with Christ – which is far better..." The Martyrs will have special crowns in Heaven for their sacrifice. I pray I don't have to receive this type of crown of martyrdom in my life, but I repeat this claim more as I get older: Jesus would be worth it.

Rapture: Could There Be More than One?

Chapter 19

REWARDS OF CROWNS

I am a huge NFL fan. Ever since my 1977 Denver Broncos made it to their first Super Bowl that ignited the city into an orange and blue frenzy with people even painting their houses those colors, I was hooked. They ultimately were humiliated by Dallas that year. Denverites swear that God created sunsets just for the Bronco fans. In those younger years, I would try to pick the winner of every NFL game with pen and paper. There was an old bookie commentator on CBS named Jimmie the Greek; I remember having a better picking percentage than he did. That obsession with football transferred over to listening to NBA games on the radio in which I could hear every cuss word that the Denver Nugget's coach Doug Moe uttered as KOA radio covered the games.

There are tale-tell moments within the professional athlete's career in which defines his time. At first, they wish to just make it on the team, especially if they are not high draft choice. If successful, they then just want to be a starter for the team, or be traded to another team who will allow them to start. They spend hours each day honing their craft to reach the goal of starting for their club. Once that plateau is reached, they set their sights on a Pro Bowl/All-Star berth to be recognized as one of the greats.

After their rookie contracts have been satisfied, the players seek the huge payday with guaranteed millions of dollars, as well as endorsement deals which can earn at least as much as their recorded salaries by the brand companies they represent. If all those goals are reached, they can be comfortable for the rest of their lives, assuming that they have good financial advice that they truly follow. Some of the best players will long for the next step. They take less money to be on the best teams to reach the real pinnacle, the championship trophy of their sport.

Now, the work goes into overdrive to refine those bad habits that have not allowed the team success. Most of the professional games are truly decided by one or two scores. It's the little things that drive them to change their game: improving their free throw percentage so that their shot is the 101-99 victory, for instance. They are seeking that crown, and once they have it, they are back in the gym or weight room sooner than a few weeks after the season to get a second trophy or atone for the loss. So it should be with Christ and our true goals of pursuit in Him: "run in such a way to win the prize" (1 Corinthians 9:24).

Good Works in Heaven

The crowns were something I had not spent any time studying in the past, because I am not sure I understood the relevance of the crowns until about a year ago. But before we may even consider the rewards, Christians need to realize that God will *not* be judging their sins. Those were judged upon the Cross of Christ, and it was truly accomplished before the "Foundation of the Earth" (Rev. 13:8).

This judgment that will occur for Believers is called

the Bema Seat of Christ (found in Revelation 4-5). The term is not well understood in today's context, because we equate judgment as an arduous process to exonerate oneself from bad decisions. Christ paid the penalty of our choices long ago. An awards banquet is a more appropriate term for the Bema Seat than a chewing out from the Lord. I wish the Church could understand this concept, so that they would look forward to this day instead of hearing the lies of the enemy that we are being judged on what we do! It's a celebration that you won't believe even if I had the ability to describe it in all of its glory.

So many Believers today have been taught that God will look into all the works of their hands, good and bad to deal with them ever so harshly. They will be weighed on the scales of justice as the American ideal stands in the courts to show that the evidence of their good outweighs the bad. But is that really true? The answer is no! God has already judged you *bad*. He has found you *not guilty*. Don't believe the lies of the enemy telling you anything different. You are the spotless Bride of Christ and the Lamb is most pleased with you because of your faith in Him. That's all you need.

The only things that will really be checked out is the difference between good things that you do for man's glory and the works you do in silent that are for your Father in Heaven. If I give away the money I mentioned earlier in this book (100 people getting one million of my billion dollars), I am given glory by the world. How can that possibly be counted by God since the glory was given by man? Ephesians 2:9 talks about our works should not be about boasting. Therefore, all the works of your hands that are truly good that no one sees are the portion that God really wants to highlight in Heaven.

White Throne Judgment

There is a judgment, on the other hand, that is referred to as the White Throne Judgment in which all non-believers from all ages will be reconstituted bodily, and then be told that they were not found in the Book of Life. The reason for this judgment is the following: while Jesus judges the Soul at the death of the unbeliever because of the consequence of his choice not to believe in Jesus' promises, but the Body hasn't been judged. The unbeliever's Body dies, but Jesus passes judgment of the Body in that last sentencing of Unbelievers to pass along His righteousness, that is given only to the Son during the White Throne Judgment.

Unbelievers should realize that we have a parallel in the world today. If someone has been suspected with enough evidence to warrant a full trial (he needs pre-hearings to realize the scope of the potential evidence), then they are sent to the County Jail until they have their trial set. This process could include years of waiting for their hearing in front of a jury. Once that jury convicts the man, he sits in the County Jail waiting for the Sentencing. After the full bore of the sentencing is completed, the man is moved to prison to stay for the balance of the sentence (albeit not considering probation and appeals).

The above process occurs for the unbeliever in a slightly different pattern. The Judge of the Universe has already found all of humanity guilty of their crime (Romans 3:23), and with the death of the Body, the Soul and Spirit spends its potential millennia in the County Jail called Hell. The White Throne Judgment then is the sentencing with the Son stating that one's name is not found in the Book of Life. Those sentenced then entering into the Lake of Fire or prison.

For the unbeliever who never makes a choice for Christ or chooses specifically against Christ, his Spirit was in death as soon as he reached the age of accountability in which he noted what Sin really meant and that he needed to make a choice for Christ. His Body lives on until he dies mortally.

His Soul is judged by the lack of a decision for Christ during his life but is only accomplished in the judgment at the time of his death. I know it seems a little complicated, because it feels as though the Body is judged at one's death, but that is not the case when it comes to Jesus' pronouncement of us. When we die, our Soul cannot make any more choices for or against Christ, because the lie of this life through Satan is that we need to do something to earn our salvation by good deeds. Some believe that we do not have to make a choice for or against Christ and live the middle road within this life. This is exactly what Satan has been trying to transmit to the unbeliever (read Ephesians 6:12-18 on how we combat Satan and his tricks).

The unbeliever's Body is then put together again with the dead Spirit and dead Soul. Those three entities of the person enter the Lake of Fire (or the above-mentioned prison) with full justice based upon Jesus' righteousness that was available to the unbeliever if he or she had only believed. But he or she chose not to take that life that was offered. Life is the only time in which that vital choice can be made. After death, those choices are so obvious that all of the deception goes away. In Heaven or Hell, deception is not needed.

Perry Stone in his Mannafest Ministries does a beautiful job at explaining the Book of Life, and it is recommended that you seek his teaching on this interesting subject. I will describe it in a more simpler way. This document says the obvious: the eternal dead do not have any life in him or her. Seems too simple?

The only inclusion I need to add here are those who are placed in Outer Darkness. Is Outer Darkness Hell? Is it an anti-chamber of Hell? We have absolutely no idea. I have watched a few ministries who have explained it (Perry Stone and Jeff Swanson Ministries), but the evidence is scant about that particular destination for potentially a thousand years or more. These would be the Goats who are false teachers. I asked a few ministry people about their feeling on the Outer Darkness and they have no real agreement, because Scripture doesn't explain it more. I think that it is *possible* that the Outer Darkness has been active for as long as humanity has had false teachers. But it is also possible that a person who is separated from his False Teaching, from the Sheep and the Goat judgment, might then enter Outer Darkness then and stay for thousands of years. It's hard to give a definitive answer on that one.

Bema Seat for Believers

But back to the Bema Seat Judgment for Believers. The crowns below represent what we may win in our pursuit of Christ. The fascinating portion of the reward is that they do not necessarily match the effort that we exert for the crown. Jesus does almost all the heavy lifting for us:

1. *Stephanos* – This is the victor's crown in which we have finished the race of our life and believed in Him (this by the way means Crown or Crowned in the Greek and is a common Eastern European name in Stephan/Stefan). It is yours to those who believe in Him (Romans 10:9-10).

2. *Incorruptible Crown* – 1 Corinthians 9:25 discusses the temporal nature of the Body versus our Heavenly Body that is a Crown in and of itself. Our Body takes on incorruption as 1 Corinthians 15 exclaims. All will receive it.

3. *Crown of Rejoicing* – This crown will be received by those who have witnessed to others for Christ. It is also given to those who have a ministry to others that made a difference in one's life for Christ. The Apostle Paul will receive this crown for the Thessalonians, but you would receive it by taking in people to minister to them during your life (Phil. 4:1 and I Thess. 2:19). Consider that rejoicing occurs in Heaven each time one comes to Christ.

4. *Crown of Life* – In Revelation 2:10, we see that by enduring the trials and temptations and overcoming those temptations, you are awarded Life. I had a partner in business who was a strong believer in Christ but struggled with alcoholism. This crown would be one of the tough areas in which I, to this day, am not sure about for my partner. Is the crown for bigger issues of life? This is a big unknown that really isn't going to be answered until the Bema Seat judgment, and I am not going to venture a guess upon it.

5. *Crown of Righteousness* – This is given for the faithfulness to use our gifts and talents, and an opportunity to serve mankind specifically which is described in

2 Timothy 4:8. I realize that most people would see this crown lining up with being the righteousness we have in Jesus, but this isn't so. Our righteousness is accomplished only from Christ, and that righteousness is given to us as a garment in Heaven. It is spoken of in Revelation 19:7-8 where Believers (the Called, Chosen and Faithful) made ready by their choice to believe Christ in His grace. God awards this when one sings in the choir, teaches a class, donates her time on a Saturday to a Church garage sale, or the even the more unknown areas of service. An example of this is Kimberly who came to sit with my mother-in-law when she was dying of Vascular Dementia in 2016, and supported my wife through this tearful time. This is the type of service we can do for our neighbors or friends, or even our enemies. It might be as simple as changing a tire or helping unload groceries from the trunk of a neighbor. All of the small things to the large things are remembered by a God who sees it all.

6. *Crown of Glory* – This one is given to those who have the specific responsibility to shepherd a people. This would come to all our worship pastors, head pastors, and staff that have direct control over a group of people. Missionaries and even children's pastors/workers would receive this diadem for their work. They would, of course, receive the Righteousness crown as well in their service, but the Glory crown comes with a lifetime of service that one gives (I Peter 5:2-4).

***

Consider these crowns as we will receive them someday. Let's say that you spent your life as a children's pastor. You might receive Righteousness and Glory. You will also have Incorruptible, Rejoicing, Stephanos and Life due to your existence upon the earth. But none of these will feel like Crowns that we have actually achieved.

I know that I will regard those Crowns with the mindset of unworthiness to receive them. I will absolutely feel the same way that if Christ had not done all the hard lifting of my life, I would not have been able to accomplish the goal of life eternal, not to mention the extra rewards. Do you now see how hard it would be to keep them on our heads with a true understanding of humility? That is what Revelation 4:10 states to us: "The 24 elders fall down before the One seated on the throne, worship the One who lives forever and ever, cast their crowns before the throne..." This is the same Scripture where a Christian band took their name, *Casting Crowns*. We will all join that band on that amazing day, casting our crowns.

Rapture: Could There Be More than One?

Chapter 20

PUTTING IT ALL TOGETHER

There is a massive amount of controversy on this topic of the Raptures. I once read a book in college about a ministry viewpoint regarding the End Times and a Post-Tribulation Rapture. As a writer myself and learning about the field of Eschatology at the time, I was disturbed by this author's misuse of the main character, an American missionary to Russia.

This fictional man was initially one of the most loving and compassionate people described in the whole book. A church in Dallas asked him to come back to America and speak to them about the happenings of the world during the Tribulation. He felt that they were already living in the Last Days. Instead the missionary went on a personal tirade about the silliness in the Church in America with people sitting in their "hidey holes" not preaching to the world about Christ's repentance, because they were waiting for the Pre-Trib Rapture that the character indicated would never come. The vehement anger displayed was completely out of character, which happens quite often in much contemporary literature when an author regularly violates their character's mentality and approach. At the end of the book, the author mentioned that he had written a thousand-page dissertation upon the Post Tribulation Rapture that went unread for the most part (Hmmm...wonder why?). He then used his fictional book of 450 pages to get his message out. Further, he went on to purport an almost guarantee that he was absolutely sure of his view that the Rapture would occur at the very end, as if he were betting his eternal salvation upon the idea.

The concept of the Post-Trib Rapture isn't new, but the venom that spews forth from many writers of that perspective is startling to the whole Church. Why are we upset at differing points of view? I attended a Church in Denver that lovingly described Churches were more like 31 flavors of ice cream, as long as they were preaching the true Gospel of the Bible, other things did not really matter. One Church utilize encouragement and another healing gifts showing forth, while another might need strong weekly teaching on the basics. There is nothing wrong with any option. Since the End Times are not spelled out as clearly as many of us would like, there must be some flexibility in the interpretation of future events.

I have held the view that I need to allow the Lord to reveal Scripture in His timing. Daniel 12:4 states "...keep these words secret and seal the book up until the time of the end. Many will roam about, and knowledge will increase." From the lips of God, we see that more revelation of the Word comes nearer the end than in centuries past. I urge all seekers of the truth to search out meanings of Scripture. Verify all that I have written here, but take all of the Word within your heart captive so that you can stand against untruth when it comes against you. Numerous sources report that human knowledge is increasing on an exponential level. I would submit that spiritual knowledge has also been snowballing in the Last Days. I believe that I am discussing just such Biblical teaching here.

My wife and I were talking about this book recently. She repeated to me Psalm 23 that has been powerful in her life. I remember singing a song of Psalm 23 in the King James Version sung by Matthew Ward in the early 1980's. The beginning of the song "Psalm 23" is acapella (without accompaniment music). "The Lord is my Shepherd I shall not want. He makes me lie down in green pastures. He leads me beside the still waters. He restoreth my soul..." I memorized the verse through the song and cannot speak the other Bible versions when I think of it.

The question sat with me for a time: is the Lord my Shepherd, hence am I His Sheep? Yes. Darrel Evans, a worship leader, sings another song "My Favorite Friend" of whom I discussed earlier. Is Jesus my favorite friend? Absolutely.

So, which is it? Is Jesus my friend or are there Friends (people who lived) who introduce the Bride to the Groom? Both. Jewish tradition teaches that the Word is like an onion in which deeper meanings can be gleaned by peeling away layers of that onion. The key to those meanings in Scripture is that the deeper meaning cannot disavow a shallower meaning. *The Lord is my Shepherd* comforts many who hear it during their darkest hours of life in which He is there to rescue us.

Most of the time, God doesn't take us away from those tough places inside of our life. He walks with us through them. He is our refuge as the Old Testament speaks of in many places. The amazing part of the Word of God is that it can be timeless and timeful. It will be timeful for those in the Tribulation who find themselves directly referred to within the Words spoken from the lips of the Almighty.

The fulfillment of the Sheep comes within those passages such as Psalms 23. The Sheep will live through the entirety of the Last Days. They will know all the horrid circumstances. Their final destiny is to walk with the Lord in green pastures when the earth is renewed in the Millennial Reign. John 10:2-9 also brings a place of remembrance for the reader on the deeper and the shallower meaning. We see that God will allow us to find that refuge in our current struggles, but the end of the verse's deep meaning is fully revealed for those who God has *Sozoed* (saved) when He shows up in the clouds (Rev. 14:16).

Throughout the Millennial Reign, if you were a part of the Bride of Christ believing in Him before the Tribulation occurred, you will be resting with Jesus, your Groom, during the whole Millennium. You will find out, if you haven't already with your partner in life (as I have with Wendy), that your lover can be your best friend. For me, I can share anything with her and converse about the small, silly things and the deeper, relational concepts of our marriage. We can debate topics with one another to sharpen the other.

Wendy is my refuge; she is my friend; she is my lover. Jesus is all to us, but He will fulfill those verses because that's what He does. He will finally finish the race with us.

I leave you with this final thought about forestalling the coming of Christ, of which cannot happen, because God has a plan for each of us and an exact time in which to do it. Revelation 9:15, as stated earlier, indicates that He has saved aside "an hour, day, month and year" for the four angels of the Sixth Trumpet to blast. He has ordered all things in Christ.

Frederick Larson of www.BethlehamStar.com does a wonderful job of proving the science within the Bible that the star at Jesus' birth truly did occur, as I detailed earlier. Mr. Larson indicates conclusively through an exhaustive research on the topic that Jesus was born on 9/11/03 BC. Does that not make you think about the terrorist event of 9/11? It has more than a decade of significance to Americans. But on that date in 3 BC, it was Rosh Hashanah. As we discovered earlier, Rosh Hashanah is the crowning of the King, their Messiah. The date significance is clear for the King to be born on Rosh Hashanah and that the Tribulation is finalized with the Last Rapture of the Called to be confirmed on that day.

The star Regulus interacted with Jupiter inside of the Leo constellation, which is known as the Lion. Jupiter orbited three times around Regulus from the perspective of Babylon, where the Wise Men could have originated 700 miles from Jerusalem. Both of those names give the ancients the concept of kingship originating within Israel. The Wise Men felt compelled to follow the sign in the stars. Mr. Larson also indicated by his research that Jesus died on a blood moon on April 3, 33 AD, in the preparation day before Passover.

He also proposed a fascinating concept within Mr. Larson's video, one that you may purchase on his website, that the God of the universe chose to set up these dates knowing that they would fulfill prophecy for the King of kings to be born and to die. He marked them before time immemorial as he flung the stars into existence.

If the Lord of Hosts gave a strong indication of the First Coming of His Son, don't you think that Jesus will come in the clouds at His Second Coming with the same purposefulness? So, He comes on the clouds at the last Rosh Hashanah for all eyes to see Him, finalizing humanity's Last Days upon the earth when He is finally crowned King of Kings. God is not without a strong sense of irony and destiny about all He does.

Rapture: Could There Be More than One?

More books to follow. Some have already come

Stay in touch with the author via:

Facebook: https://www.facebook.com/Dr-Scott-Young/

Twitter: https://twitter.com/DrScottYoung.

Website: www.DrScottYoung.com

Rapture: Could There Be More than One?

ABOUT THE AUTHOR

Dr. Scott Young, CCC-A, FAAA, an Audiologist since 1991 and owns Hearing Solution Centers, Inc. in Tulsa, OK. Besides World War II studies, his passions include writing, Sci-Fi and singing. He has written a fictional novel, *The Violin's Secret*, which chronicles the survival of one young teenager through the Holocaust. *Singing in the Mind: A Study of the Voice and Song* was his first non-fictional writing about the passion of singing and a different view of how singing occurs in the mind and its role in culture.

Professor in History was his third, but second fictional, book of a man who is an atheist but has the amazing opportunity to ask Jesus unique questions on various topics. *ForeTold - Book 1 and 2* will be out soon enough chronicling the End of the Earth from a Biblical perspective in a fictional form.

More information can be found at www.DrScottYoung.com. Dr. Young is a unique communicator in the way he perceives the world as his wife, Wendy, and his son, Stefan, will attest. My thanks goes to Wendy and Stefan who read this book quite thoroughly to find my errors.

Bible Verse on HSCB (Holmann's)

PRE-TRIBULATION RAPTURE (as well as types and models of it):

I Cor. 15:20	Gen. 5:24	Tit. 2:13
I John 3:3	I Thess. 4:16	John 20:17
I Thess. 5:9	Gal. 1:4	Luke 12:42
Luke 19:13	Luke 21:36	Rev. 3:3-10
Matt. 24:40-46	Rev. 4:1	Gen. 5:24
Matt. 16:28	Matt. 25:10	Phil. 3:21

MID-TRIBULATION RAPTURE:

2 Pet. 2:9	Luke 12:38	Matt. 22:11
Matt. 22:14	Rev. 14:1-3	Rev. 7:9
Matt. 24:31	Mark 13:27	Rom. 5:10

POST-TRIBULATION RAPTURE:

I Thess. 1:10	2 Pet. 3:9-10	2 Thess.1:10
Ex. 21:6	Luke 12:37	Luke 9:27
Mark 13:27	Matt. 24:13	Matt. 24:30

Rev. 14:14-16   1 Cor. 15:52   2 Thess. 1:10

Luke 9:27   1 Cor. 15:21   Rev. 19:9

James 5:7

CALLED:

I Thess. 1:6	Luke 12:47	Luke 14:23
Rev. 14:17	Luke 14:6	Rev. 14:6
Mark 13:9	John 14:2	Rom. 8:28
2 Tit. 1:9	Rom. 1:1	2 John 1:8

CHOSEN:

I Cor. 3:10	Luke 12:48	Mark 13:20
Matt. 24:22	Rev. 7:15	1 Cor. 3:10
Matt. 24:24	Rom. 8:29	Rom. 8:33
Rom. 11:7	2 Tim. 2:10	Tit. 1:1
2 Pet. 1:10	Rev. 7:15	

FAITHFUL:

I Cor. 4:2	Acts 1:7	Rev. 3:21
1 Cor. 6:3	Mark 2:21	Eph. 5
Ex. 22:17	Song Sol. 4:9	Matt. 25:5

Acts 2:17   I Pet. 3:21   Rev. 21:2

Rev. 22:17

GOATS:

I Cor. 3:17	John 15:6	Luke 12:48
Luke 13:26	Luke 3:9	Luke 6:49
Luke 8:18	Matt. 22:8	Matt. 23:39
Matt. 24:10	Matt. 25:10	Matt. 25:25
Matt. 25:32	Matt. 25:41	Matt. 7:21
Rev. 16:15	Rev. 3:18	(Many more)

SHEEP:

I Cor. 3:13-15	Exo. 21:2	John 10:16
John 10:2-9	Matt. 25:34-46	Rev. 14:14
Rev. 14:9	Rev. 19:15	Zach.14:16-17
Dan. 4:25	Ezk. 34:23	Joel 2:32
Matt. 24:40		

Made in the USA
Coppell, TX
24 October 2019

10383596R00089